WITH HIS BELOVED RESTAURANTS
Pickle, Tiffin and Street, award-winning chef Sunil Ghai has revolutionized Indian cooking in Ireland.

Sunil fell in love with cooking while helping his mother, an exceptional home cook. He completed his training as a chef at the prestigious five-star Oberoi Hotel Group in India before moving to Dublin in 2000. When it opened in 2016, his restaurant, Pickle, was an immediate sensation for its authentic home-style north Indian food.

Now, in his first cookbook, *Spice Box*, Sunil shares his uncomplicated approach to making delicious Indian food at home using readily available ingredients.

Sunil lives with his family in Greystones, Co. Wicklow.

SPICE BOX

EASY, EVERYDAY INDIAN FOOD

SPICE BOX

EASY, EVERYDAY INDIAN FOOD

SUNIL GHAI
WITH **KRISTIN JENSEN**

Photography by Joanne Murphy

PENGUIN
SANDYCOVE

AN IMPRINT OF
PENGUIN BOOKS

Dedicated to my beloved father, Shri Guru Dutt Ghai

CONTENTS

Foreword 8
Introduction 10

CHAPTER 1 Chicken 20

CHAPTER 2 Pork, lamb and goat 52

CHAPTER 3 Seafood 94

CHAPTER 4 Vegetarian mains 124

CHAPTER 5 Salads, sides and snacks 164

CHAPTER 6 Rice and bread 202

CHAPTER 7 Chutneys and raitas 220

CHAPTER 8 Desserts and drinks 238

Index 264
Acknowledgements 270

FOREWORD

By Rajiv Gulshan and Darina Allen

Sunil was only 21 years old, a polite young Gwalior boy, when I met him in the kitchen of the Cecil, an Oberoi Hotel in the Himalayas. Dreamy-eyed, handsome and always in impeccable uniform, Sunil won the guests' hearts through his uncanny ability to convert local Himalayan ingredients into spectacular salads and appetisers. His ability to combine various flavours and create a masterpiece was also recognised by the rest of the brigade and the management.

When it came to the food served in Indian restaurants before Sunil arrived in Dublin, it was never what we ate at home in India. At best, I can describe the food served in that period as greasy, oily, unnaturally colourful and heavy. Sunil demonstrated grit and determination to stand up and claim back the 'Indian-ness' of his cuisine. Due to his collaborative nature, he was able to work closely with another giant of authentic Indian cuisine, Asheesh Dewan of Jaipur and Ananda fame, and Atul Kochhar, a Michelin-starred chef from London, to bring about this change.

This book is an almanac of authentic, time-tested recipes gathered from the shepherd families in the Himalayas to the royal families of Gwalior, Punjab and Jaipur – all perfected by Sunil and his wife, Leena, in their home kitchen in Dublin. The flow of the book is easy to follow and allows both novice cooks and experts to stock their kitchen with the right ingredients to cook authentically.

I am sure you will enjoy cooking the recipes from this book. The words 'Satyameva Jayate' (Truth Alone Triumphs) are proudly displayed on the wall of Pickle, Sunil's Camden Street restaurant. This book is a true representation of Sunil's personal quest for that tantalising balance in reverence of traditional, time-honoured fundamentals of Indian cuisine, set ablaze by his creativity and grounded innovation.

Rajiv Gulshan, Dean of Le Cordon Bleu School of Hospitality, Gurgaon, India

My first bite of Sunil's food, back when he was cooking at Ananda in Dundrum in the early 2000s, stopped me mid-sentence. I was curious – who exactly was the chef behind these delicious flavours? Then Sunil Ghai emerged from the kitchen.

Up until then, Indian food on restaurant menus on this side of the world seemed far from authentic and rarely reflected the diversity of flavours I'd enjoyed in India. For decades I've travelled widely in India, loving the variety of food, from street stalls and dhabas to restaurant and hotel kitchens. Most of all, I loved the home cooking when we were fortunate enough to be invited into people's houses.

I've been lucky to eat Sunil's food on many occasions since then and have invited him to teach at the Ballymaloe Cookery School and to participate in the Ballymaloe LitFest. Over and over again, I encouraged him to write a book to share his cooking, not just with his many devotees, but with a wider audience who would love to be able to cook delicious, authentic Indian food, particularly the kind of home cooking, often with a contemporary twist, that Sunil and his team serve at his restaurants Pickle, Tiffin and Street.

And at last, here it is – an accessible introduction to Indian food using spices that are widely available at supermarkets around the country, illustrating that anyone can make authentic Indian food with ingredients that can be sourced locally. I couldn't wait to flick through this book to find the secret to many of my favourite recipes and discover so much more.

Sunil is a master of spices, using them to layer flavour in food and make it come alive. In this book, he shows you how to create those same layers of flavour. He also outlines his foolproof formula for how to make curry. You will be amazed at how using the same techniques but with different spices and ingredients will give you endless variations and many delicious meals. If you can make a Bolognese sauce, you can make any of these curries.

Thank you, Sunil, for sharing your passion, for taking the mystery out of Indian food and for introducing us to so many irresistible dishes so that each and every one of us can create an Indian feast at home.

Darina Allen, Ballymaloe Cookery School, Cork, Ireland

INTRODUCTION

Indian food isn't spicy – it's full of spice. It's not all about chillies and heat; it's about building layers of flavour. Contrary to what many people think, you don't need to buy dozens of spices or make a special trip to an Asian shop to cook Indian food at home. This book will show you that you can create authentic Indian dishes using spices and ingredients that can be found in any supermarket.

In India, a spice box is called namak dani and every household has one. It's a round tin containing smaller round canisters within it that keep the spices separate while still giving you easy access. Every family will have their own mix in their spice box. The recipes in this book use the spices that I cook with at home: bay leaves, cinnamon, cloves, coriander, cumin, dried red chillies, fennel seeds, garam masala, green cardamom pods, ground mace or nutmeg, mustard seeds, nigella seeds, paprika, red chilli flakes, saffron, star anise and turmeric.

Going back to basics

Before I opened my first restaurant, Pickle, in 2016 on Camden Street in Dublin, I was cooking formal, modern, fusion-style Indian food at Ananda in Dundrum, so the home-style food I cook at Pickle is a big change from that. Most of the recipes in this book come from my childhood in northern India – my mother's cooking is my biggest influence – and from Pickle. As such, they're a mix of traditional favourites and newer dishes with more contemporary twists. But this is not restaurant food. I want this book to give you the chance to cook something different and delicious for you and your family and friends, so all the recipes are easy to make at home. Many of them also have the added advantage of being suitable for batch cooking – in fact, curries taste even better the day after they're made – helping you to get ahead on busy days.

Authentic Indian food at home

When I moved to Ireland in 2000 there were already plenty of Indian restaurants here, so I visited as many as I could to see what was being offered. Why were people so obsessed with only lamb or chicken korma rather than a home-style chicken curry? Why were people eating only chicken breasts, not thighs? Why were people being served chicken tikka that was a strange, lurid beetroot colour rather than a chilli-red tandoori chicken on the bone?

Many people's idea of Indian food has been based on the food they've been served in restaurants, but oftentimes that food has been altered to cater for

Western tastes and is not a true representation of authentic Indian food. In my restaurants I'm trying to change that, but it took me and my team a long time to bring people along and help them understand what real Indian food should be.

In my experience, rather than trying to educate the customer, Indian chefs would just give them what they wanted. It's similar to the way many Chinese restaurants in Ireland serve dishes that bear little resemblance to real Chinese food the way it's served in China. These dishes have been modified to cater for Irish tastes, which veer to the sweet side of the spectrum. It's not really Chinese food; it's something else.

The same is true of much of the Indian food that's served in Ireland. People always ask me why I don't have lamb rogan josh on my menu. I know how to make it, of course, but many people would be hesitant to eat it if I put a bowl of proper rogan josh in front of them, with a layer of oil floating on top and a thin, not thick, base. I could serve what people have come to expect, but I don't want to confuse people with watered-down versions of authentic dishes.

When I worked in a restaurant in Malahide in County Dublin, I would know if a particular couple was sitting in the restaurant based on the order that came through: two chicken tikka starters, two chicken kormas, one Peshwari naan, one plain naan. Every week I felt more and more frustrated by that order, so finally I went out to their table and asked why they were eating the same thing all the time. The man said that korma was all he'd ever had and it was what he liked. I went back into the kitchen and made him the korma, but I also sent out two bowls of curry – the home-style curry we made for the staff meal and a butter chicken curry. After a while the waiter said the man was asking for me. He loved the butter chicken, though the curry was too rustic for him. 'Next time,' he said, 'I'm ordering the butter chicken.' That's how you change people's perceptions. If I hadn't gone out and talked to them and sent out those other dishes, he never would have tried anything else.

But people are more adventurous now in terms of what they're willing to try and they also want to know more about the cuisine. When it gets to the point where someone becomes a regular and I know who's eating in the restaurant based on the order that comes in time and time again, I'll go out and talk to them and encourage them to try something new. And I very often change people's minds, whether it's getting them to try a different type of curry or even something they may never have had before, like my signature dish of goat on toast. With the easy, everyday recipes in this book, I hope that I can encourage you, too, to cook something new using ingredients you're already familiar with.

STOCKING YOUR SPICE BOX AND CUPBOARDS

All the recipes in this book use widely available everyday ingredients, such as basmati rice, lemons and limes, fresh herbs and Greek yoghurt. You probably have some of them in your fridge or cupboards already. It used to be hard to find unusual ingredients in Irish supermarkets, but now things like coconut oil and pomegranates are widely available because the demand for them is there. Avonmore is even making a pure Irish ghee now (ghee is a clarified butter with a high smoke point, which makes it better suited to frying and roasting).

Don't be put off if at first glance a recipe looks like it has a long ingredients list – spices take no time to prepare, just a minute to measure out. Asian shops tend to have a wider selection of spices and are better value than the supermarkets (I like the East End brand for their good, clean flavours), but the spices you can get in any supermarket or well-stocked grocery shop will still be delicious.

ESSENTIAL SPICE BOX

- Bay leaves
- Cinnamon (sticks and ground)
- Cloves (whole and ground)
- Coriander (seeds and ground)
- Cumin (seeds and ground)
- Dried red chillies (I use Kashmiri chillies but you can substitute fresh red ones)
- Fennel seeds
- Garam masala
- Green cardamom pods
- Ground mace (or nutmeg)
- Ground turmeric
- Mustard seeds
- Nigella seeds
- Paprika
- Red chilli flakes
- Saffron
- Star anise

PANTRY STAPLES

- Almond or cashew butter
- Basmati rice
- Chickpeas
- Chutney
- Coconut milk
- Coconut oil
- Garlic
- Lentils and split peas
- Nuts (almonds, cashews, pistachios, walnuts)
- Onions (white and red)
- Tinned chopped tomatoes
- Tomato passata (ideally in a jar, not a carton)
- Tomato purée
- Vegetable and rapeseed oil

FRESH FOOD

- Butter or ghee (clarified butter)
- Fresh herbs: basil, coriander, dill, mint
- Ginger
- Green and red chillies
- Lemons and limes
- Yoghurt (Greek and natural)

GETTING THE MOST OUT OF YOUR INGREDIENTS AND SPICES

I believe that it's not the skill of the chef, but rather the ingredients you use that determine the success of a recipe. You could be the most talented cook, but if your fish isn't fresh, what can you do about it? If your chillies aren't spicy, you can't make them spicier. In Ireland we are lucky to have such excellent local and artisan produce, while Irish lamb is the best that I have ever cooked with. These recipes are simple, but buying the best, freshest ingredients you can and treating your spices well will make a world of difference.

- Keep your spices in airtight jars in a cool, dark place for no longer than six months. Don't use old spices or spices that have been open for a long time. The spices that have been in the back of your cupboard since who knows when won't have any flavour – get rid of them.
- In my restaurants, we toast and grind all our own whole spices (except when they are being added directly to hot oil, in which case it's not necessary to toast them first). You'll get delicious results using ready-ground spices, but if you want to get the maximum flavour, I always recommend that you buy whole spices and grind them yourself in small quantities. This not only gives you the best, freshest flavour, but whole spices also have a longer shelf life than ground. To take things one step further, toast your whole spices in a hot, dry, heavy-based pan just until they're aromatic or start to crackle and pop, then tip them out on to a plate and allow to cool to room temperature before grinding in a coffee grinder.
- I wanted all the recipes in this book to use spices that you can easily find in any supermarket, such as paprika. However, if you have access to an Asian market and want to create an even more authentic flavour, you can use the equivalent amount of Kashmiri chilli powder anywhere you see paprika listed in the ingredients (look for the Deggi Mirch brand of chilli powder).
- The best way to peel ginger is with the edge of a small metal spoon rather than with a vegetable peeler.
- Use a Microplane rasp grater to grate garlic and ginger. When grating garlic this way you don't even need to peel the cloves, as their papery skins will flake away on their own when you grate it.
- To make your fresh herbs last longer, wash and dry them in a salad spinner on the day that you buy them, then store them in an airtight container lined with a piece of kitchen paper. Not only will they stay fresher for longer this way, but the fact that they're already washed and dried makes them easier for you to use in your cooking.

HOW TO USE THIS BOOK

There are three keys to success with the recipes in this book: measuring and preparing all your spices and ingredients before you start cooking; understanding how the spices are used to layer flavours; and understanding the basic curry formula.

Measure and prepare all your spices and ingredients

Before you start cooking, measure all your spices into small bowls. You will usually need one bowl for the whole spices, one for the dried spices to add to the curry sauce and perhaps a third bowl for the finishing spices to add at the very end.

Doing this at the start means that nothing is in danger of burning, as spices generally need to be cooked for only 1 or 2 minutes. This is similar to the way you should have all your stir-fry ingredients prepped and ready to go before you start cooking, as everything cooks and comes together so quickly.

Prepping first will also make cooking these recipes much more relaxed. Instead of rushing to measure spices or chop onions, follow the prep instructions at the start of every recipe. This is what chefs call mise en place and it's not just for spices. Spend 10 minutes peeling and chopping the onions, ginger and garlic and measuring and preparing all the other ingredients before you begin to cook and you will be amazed at how quickly and easily the recipes come together, with plenty of time to clean up as you go. You can have a delicious homemade curry simmering on the hob and have the kitchen tidied up too by the time you sit down to dinner.

I promise you that prepping everything first will completely change your experience of cooking not just my recipes, but all your cooking. You can get inexpensive prep bowls from catering companies – try the Arcoroc range of chef bowls from Nisbets in Dublin, which come in different sizes that are stackable in your cupboard.

Understand how the spices are used

Spices are typically used in three different ways in this book, with all three methods often used in the same recipe:

1. Add whole spices to hot oil at the start of the cooking.
2. Add ground spices before adding any liquid.
3. Add a pinch of ground spices at the end of the cooking time.

Whole spices are added to hot oil at the start of the cooking to release their bold flavours and any oils that the spices themselves may contain. This is called tempering the spices. When you cook spices in hot oil, they lose their heat, whereas when you dry-roast them, the heat becomes more pronounced. Cooking chillies in oil reduces the heat and makes them much milder by coating them in fat and wicking away the moisture. And speaking of chillies, I often add whole fresh chillies, halved lengthways, to a dish rather than chopping them. This way, you get all the flavour and a subtle warmth without ever biting into the chilli itself.

I almost always add a splash of water when I add the ground spices so that the spices don't burn, because usually there is no other liquid in the pan at that point. Ground spices such as garam masala are often used to finish a curry by enhancing the flavours at the very end.

Understand the basic curry formula
Once you've made a few curries from this book, you'll see how formulaic they actually are. Most of them follow the same four steps:
1. Temper the whole spices in hot oil for 1 minute, just until fragrant or the whole seeds start to pop.
2. Cook the onions and fresh green chillies (if using) with the salt until softened (the salt helps to draw out the water in the onions), then add the ginger and garlic and cook for 1–2 minutes more, just until fragrant.
3. Add the protein and sauce ingredients, such as coconut milk, Greek yoghurt, tomato passata and/or water, and let the curry simmer to marry the flavours together. I use a lot of water in my recipes, not stock, as there is plenty of flavour from the other ingredients. I've put the water in bold in the recipes so that you don't accidentally skip over or forget this vital ingredient.
4. Finish the dish with a final pinch of ground spice, fresh herbs, a knob of butter, a little cream and/or a squeeze of lemon juice.

This is why we've laid out the recipes the way we have in this book – you can see at a glance which ingredients belong with which step. This is also why your mise en place (measuring and prepping all your ingredients before you start cooking) is so helpful and makes cooking these recipes so easy.

How to deep-fry without a deep-fryer
Several of the recipes in this book require deep-frying, but if you don't have a dedicated deep-fryer it is still possible to cook them following these tips.
- Use a large, wide, deep-sided, heavy-based saucepan or casserole.
- Make sure your pan and utensils are dry before you start to cook. If your food

is not coated, crumbed or battered, pat it dry with a piece of kitchen paper too. Oil and water do not mix, so any water in or on the pan, utensils or the food itself could cause the hot oil to 'spit' and possibly burn you.
- Do not fill the pan more than half-full with oil. If you overfill the pan, the hot oil might spill over the sides once you add the food.
- A kitchen thermometer (e.g. a candy thermometer) clipped to the side of the pan is the best way to measure the temperature of the oil, but if you don't have one you can gauge the temperature using a wooden spoon or chopstick. Put the tip of the wooden spoon or chopstick in the hot oil – if bubbles start forming around it, the oil is hot enough for frying. Alternatively, you can drop a cube of white bread or a slice of onion into the oil – if the bread turns golden brown and crisp in 45–60 seconds or if the onion immediately starts to sizzle, the oil is ready.
- Use long-handled tongs, a slotted spoon or a spider for removing the cooked food from the hot oil.
- When frying, make sure the kitchen is well ventilated and keep children away from the hob.

I use ginger and garlic in many recipes, so it will be helpful to know the following:

1 tbsp grated or finely chopped ginger = 1 thumb-sized piece of peeled fresh ginger
1 tbsp grated or finely chopped garlic = 2 or 3 large peeled garlic cloves

CHAPTER 1

★

CHICKEN

SERVES **4** TO **6**

— MURGH RASEDAR —
HOME-STYLE CHICKEN CURRY

I learned this recipe from chef Atul Kochhar in London, who used to teach classes at the Dublin Cookery School, where I would assist him. He uses spices so masterfully and I learned a lot from him. This is the simplest curry recipe I know, but there's nothing better.

PREP

Measure out your spices into three separate small bowls: one bowl for the whole spices; one for the coriander, turmeric and paprika for the curry; and one for the garam masala to finish.

Prep and measure out all the remaining ingredients before you start cooking so that everything is ready to go and the spices don't burn.

SERVES **6** TO **8**

— MURGH MALAI KEBABS —
CARDAMOM AND SAFFRON CHICKEN KEBABS

This is the most famous, simplest kebab, served all throughout India. When I was doing my training back in 1993 at the Mughal Sheraton Agra hotel in their Chinese kitchen, Mahjong, I would go to the Indian kitchen during my breaks. The head chef there would ask me what I wanted to eat and I always asked for this kebab, which I'd have with naan and yellow dal. I loved it then and it's still one of my favourites.

SERVES **4** AS A SIDE

— FAUZI KADAK PANKHURI —
OVEN-ROASTED CHICKEN WINGS

My brother-in-law is a lieutenant colonel in the Indian Army and he always eats in the army mess to make sure the food is good enough for his troops. One time when I was visiting him, I went to eat with him there and these chicken wings were on the menu. I loved them, so I got the recipe from the chefs there (fauzi means army man or soldier, so I've called them that in honour of the mess hall chefs and soldiers). I put them on my own menu at Pickle, where we serve them as chicken lollipops. Oven-baked chicken wings are much faster and easier to do at home, but you could look up videos online of how to lollipop the wings. Toss them in 2 tablespoons of cornflour and deep-fry them for about 5 minutes if you want to make them like we do in the restaurant.

MARINATE THE CHICKEN

1–2 fresh green chillies, finely chopped

1 tbsp grated or finely chopped fresh ginger

1 tbsp grated or finely chopped garlic

20g fresh coriander, stems chopped (reserve the leaves for another dish or for garnish)

1 tbsp paprika

1 tsp ground cumin

1 tsp ground black pepper

½ tsp fine sea salt

juice of 1 lemon

4 tbsp vegetable oil

1kg chicken wings

Make the marinade by mixing the green chillies, ginger, garlic, coriander stems, spices, salt, lemon juice and oil in a medium bowl.

Add the chicken wings, stirring to coat them all in the marinade. Cover the bowl with cling film and marinate in the fridge for at least 30 minutes, but preferably a few hours or overnight, to marry the flavours together.

COOK THE CHICKEN

Preheat the oven to 240°C/220°C fan/gas 9. Line a large baking tray with foil.

Place the wings on the lined tray in a single layer, shaking off any large clumps of excess marinade so it doesn't scorch in the hot oven. Cook in the preheated oven for 30–40 minutes, until the wings are cooked through and the skin is crisp. Season with a little salt and pepper once they come out of the oven.

To serve Serve with a bowl of tomato and cashew chutney (page 222) or your favourite shop-bought chutney on the side for dipping.

SERVES **4** TO **6**

— MURGH MUGHLAI —
LUCKNOWI CHICKEN CURRY

This delicately flavoured and subtly perfumed dish is a type of korma that's popular with Muslims in Lucknow, a large city in northern India. It's usually eaten with equally fragrant rice perfumed with rosewater and kewra water. Kewra water is a floral water that's similar to rosewater, but it's made from pandanus flowers. It's a classic northern Indian flavouring.

PREP

Measure out your spices into two separate small bowls: one bowl for the whole spices and one for the ground coriander, cumin, paprika and turmeric for the curry.

Prep and measure out all the remaining ingredients before you start cooking so that everything is ready to go and the spices don't burn.

COOK THE WHOLE SPICES

50g butter or ghee

50ml vegetable oil

8 green cardamom pods

3–4 cloves

3 bay leaves

1 cinnamon stick

1 tsp cumin seeds

Heat the butter or ghee and the oil in a large heavy-based saucepan over a medium heat. Add the cardamom, cloves, bay leaves, cinnamon stick and cumin seeds and cook for 1 minute, until fragrant.

MAKE THE CURRY

1 large onion, thinly sliced (200g)

1¼ tsp fine sea salt

1 tbsp grated or finely chopped fresh ginger

1 tbsp grated or finely chopped garlic

500g boneless, skinless chicken thighs or breasts, cut into large pieces (50g)

1½ tbsp ground coriander

1 tsp ground cumin

1 tsp paprika

½ tsp ground turmeric

50g thick Greek yoghurt

1 small ripe tomato, chopped

pinch of saffron, soaked in 20ml cream

Add the onion and salt and cook for about 10 minutes, until golden brown. Add the ginger and garlic and cook for 1 minute more, just until fragrant.

Add the chicken and cook for 1 minute just to seal, then add the ground spices and **50ml water** so that the spices don't burn. Stir in the yoghurt and tomato and cook for 1–2 minutes, then stir in another **200ml water**. Simmer for a few minutes, then add the saffron-infused cream. Simmer gently for 15–20 minutes, until the chicken is tender and cooked through. Remove the pan from the heat and allow the curry to settle for 5 minutes.

To serve Serve with plain boiled basmati rice (page 204) and warm naan (shop-bought or page 211).

1. COOK THE WHOLE SPICES

6 green cardamom pods

4 cloves

2 tsp cumin seeds

100ml vegetable oil

1 cinnamon stick

1 bay leaf

Put the cardamom, cloves and cumin seeds in a pestle and mortar and lightly crush them. If you don't have a pestle and mortar, you can crush the whole spices with a rolling pin instead.

Heat the oil in a large heavy-based saucepan over a medium heat. Add the crushed spices, cinnamon stick and bay leaf and cook for 1 minute, until fragrant.

2. MAKE THE CURRY

2 medium onions, thinly sliced (250g)

1½ tsp fine sea salt

2 tbsp grated or finely chopped fresh ginger

2 tbsp grated or finely chopped garlic

1½ tbsp ground coriander

1½ tsp ground turmeric

1½ tsp paprika

1 tbsp tomato purée

100g tomato passata

600g boneless, skinless chicken thighs or breasts, cut into large pieces (50g)

Add the onions and salt and cook for about 10 minutes, until softened but not browned. Add the ginger and garlic and cook for 1 minute more.

Add the ground coriander, turmeric and paprika, then stir in **50ml water** so that the spices don't burn. Add the tomato purée and cook for 1 minute, stirring, then add the passata. Cook for about 5 minutes, until the fat starts to separate out from the sauce at the edge of the pan. Add the chicken along with another **300ml water**.

Bring to the boil, then reduce the heat to low and simmer for 20–25 minutes, until the chicken is completely cooked through, topping up with a little more water if the sauce has reduced too much.

3. TO FINISH

8 cherry tomatoes, halved

1 tbsp chopped fresh coriander, plus extra to garnish

¼ tsp garam masala

Stir in the cherry tomatoes, chopped fresh coriander and garam masala. Remove the pan from the heat and allow the curry to settle for 5 minutes.

To serve Garnish with a little chopped fresh coriander, then serve with plain boiled basmati rice (page 204) and warm naan (shop-bought or page 211).

MAKE THE FIRST MARINADE

4 green cardamom pods

juice of 1 small lime

2 fresh green chillies, finely chopped

1 tbsp grated or finely chopped fresh ginger

1 tbsp grated or finely chopped garlic

1 tsp fine sea salt

8 skinless chicken breasts, cut into large pieces (50g each)

Crush the cardamom pods to a powder in a pestle and mortar, then tip out into a large bowl. Add the lime juice, green chillies, ginger, garlic and salt and mix together, then add the chicken and stir to coat. Leave to sit for 20–30 minutes while you prepare the second marinade.

MAKE THE SECOND MARINADE

120g mascarpone cheese (or cream cheese)

120g thick Greek yoghurt

120ml double cream

1 tbsp chopped fresh coriander

½ tsp fine sea salt

squeeze of lime juice

pinch of saffron

Whisk together all the ingredients for the second marinade in a separate large bowl until smooth and thick.

Squeeze the chicken pieces in your hands before you transfer them to the bowl with the second marinade – you don't want any liquid from the first marinade to thin the second one, as you want the thick, creamy marinade to stick to the chicken. Stir to coat the chicken in the second marinade. Cover the bowl with cling film and marinate in the fridge for at least 30 minutes, but preferably 2–3 hours or overnight.

COOK THE KEBABS

large knob of butter, melted

Preheat the oven to 220°C/200°C fan/gas 7.

Remove the chicken from the marinade and thread on to six to eight metal skewers. Place the skewers on one or two large baking trays and cook in the preheated oven for about 10 minutes. Remove the trays from the oven, baste the chicken with the melted butter and return to the oven to cook for a further 10 minutes, until the chicken is completely cooked through. Remove from the oven and baste again with any remaining butter.

To serve Serve the kebabs hot with a little shredded fresh mint scattered over and some mint and coriander chutney (page 224), pickled red onions (page 200) and lemon wedges on the side.

SERVES **4** TO **6**

— MURGH KALI MIRCH —
BLACK PEPPER CHICKEN CURRY

Black pepper works wonderfully in Indian dishes in combination with other spices. This curry is typical of ones from southern India, where they use a lot of black spices like black pepper, black cardamom and cloves. This is a very thick curry and very spicy, so it's one for people who like a lot of heat. However, black pepper doesn't work like chilli heat – it gives you a different sensation. It can be quite numbing, but it's also addictive: it's hot, but you can't stop eating it.

PREP

Measure out your spices into three separate small bowls: one bowl for the whole spices; one for the ground black pepper, cumin and coriander for the curry; and one for the salt to finish.

Prep and measure out all the remaining ingredients before you start cooking so that everything is ready to go and the spices don't burn.

 ## COOK THE WHOLE SPICES

60ml vegetable oil

25 whole black peppercorns

6 green cardamom pods

2 star anise

1–2 bay leaves

1 cinnamon stick

1 tbsp cumin seeds

Heat the oil in a large heavy-based saucepan over a medium heat. Add the peppercorns, cardamom, star anise, bay leaves, cinnamon stick and cumin seeds. Cook for 1 minute, until fragrant.

 ## MAKE THE CURRY

1 large onion, thinly sliced (200g)

1½ tsp fine sea salt

3 fresh green chillies, halved lengthways

1 tbsp grated or finely chopped fresh ginger

1 tbsp grated or finely chopped garlic

2 heaped tbsp ground black pepper

1 heaped tbsp ground cumin

1 heaped tbsp ground coriander

200g tomato passata or 1 x 227g tin of chopped tomatoes

500g boneless, skinless chicken thighs or breasts, cut into large pieces (50g)

Add the onion and salt and cook for about 10 minutes, until softened and golden brown. Add the green chillies, ginger and garlic and cook for 1 minute before adding the ground black pepper, cumin and coriander along with **50ml water** so that the spices don't burn. Cook for 1–2 minutes.

Add the tomatoes and cook for a few minutes more, still stirring. Add the chicken and stir to coat, then add another **400ml water**. Cover the pan, reduce the heat and simmer for about 20 minutes, until the chicken is completely cooked through.

Remove the lid, bring to the boil and cook until the liquid has reduced – this curry is meant to be very thick.

TO FINISH

½ tsp fine sea salt

25g fresh coriander, chopped, plus extra to garnish

Season with another ½ teaspoon of salt (or to taste) and stir in the chopped fresh coriander. Remove the pan from the heat and allow the curry to settle for 5 minutes.

To serve Garnish with a little chopped fresh coriander, then serve with plain boiled basmati rice (page 204) and warm naan (shop-bought or page 211).

SERVES 4

— PUNJABI MURGH MAKHANI —
EASY BUTTER CHICKEN

When people order butter chicken in my restaurants I assume that they know the dish has butter and cream in it, yet I once had a customer tell me he didn't want any butter in his butter chicken. (I suggested he have a curry instead.) When I was doing my training in India, one of my first jobs was to melt 4 kilograms of unsalted butter so that the chef could use it to baste the chicken. This dish is meant to have plenty of fat and rich flavours. It's our bestselling dish by far.

> **PREP**
>
> Measure out your spices into two separate bowls: one medium bowl for the paprika and salt for the marinade and one small bowl for the paprika and salt for the sauce.
>
> Prep and measure out all the remaining ingredients before you start cooking so that everything is ready to go and the spices don't burn.

MARINATE THE CHICKEN

80g thick Greek yoghurt

1 tbsp grated or finely chopped fresh ginger

1 tbsp grated or finely chopped garlic

1 tsp paprika

½ tsp fine sea salt

750g boneless, skinless chicken thighs or breasts, cut into large pieces (50g)

Put the yoghurt, ginger, garlic, paprika and salt in a medium bowl and mix to combine, then add the chicken pieces and stir to coat. Cover the bowl with cling film and leave out on the counter to marinate for 20–30 minutes while you make the sauce (or even better, let it marinate in the fridge overnight).

2 COOK THE CHICKEN

large knob of butter, melted

Preheat the oven to 220°C/200°C fan/gas 7.

Transfer the chicken to a baking tray and spread out the pieces in a single layer. Cook in the preheated oven for 8–10 minutes, until almost cooked through.

Remove from the oven and brush with the melted butter, then set aside.

3 MAKE THE SAUCE

125g butter

1–2 fresh green chillies, halved lengthways

1 tbsp grated or finely chopped fresh ginger

1 tbsp grated or finely chopped garlic

1 tsp paprika

½ tsp fine sea salt

1 tbsp cashew butter

1 x 700g jar of tomato passata

100ml cream

Meanwhile, to make the sauce, melt the butter in a large heavy-based saucepan over a low heat. Add the green chillies, ginger and garlic and cook for 1 minute, until fragrant. Stir in the paprika and salt and cook for 1 minute, then stir in the cashew butter.

Add the passata and stir to combine, then add the chicken, increase the heat to medium and simmer for 20–30 minutes, until the flavours have combined and the sauce has reduced a bit. Add the cream and simmer for 1–2 minutes, then taste and adjust the seasoning if needed. Remove and discard the green chilli halves. Remove the pan from the heat and allow the curry to settle for 5 minutes.

To serve Ladle the curry into warmed bowls on top of plain boiled basmati rice (page 204). Add a spoonful of Greek yoghurt on top of each bowl and garnish with a pinch of paprika. Serve with warm naan on the side (shop-bought or page 211).

SERVES **6** TO **8**

— MURGH QORMA —
CHICKEN KORMA

This is one of the most confusing dishes you can put on your menu because people have so many different expectations of what a korma is. You could go to five different Indian restaurants and the korma will be different in each one. In some places the sauce will be thick and lumpy, while other restaurants add raisins. I wanted to do a korma, but I wanted to make it more authentic. A proper northern Indian korma can't be made without nuts and is always made with chicken on the bone. Traditionally it's quite rich thanks to the nuts, browned onions, butter, cream and saffron, but it's not meant to be an everyday dish – it's for a special occasion. I use Greek yoghurt to lighten it a bit.

The sauce is the most important part of a korma. I'm using chicken in this basic recipe, but you could use vegetables or lamb instead – use almonds instead of cashews to stand up to the strong flavour of lamb and add some fresh mint too.

PREP

If you soak the cashews in a bowl of cold water beforehand (for as little as 30 minutes or up to overnight) it will speed up the cooking time when you add them to the sauce, but it's not necessary to do this.

Measure out your spices into three separate small bowls: one bowl for the whole spices; one for the cumin, turmeric and mace or nutmeg for the korma sauce; and one for the pinch of saffron to finish.

Prep and measure out all the remaining ingredients before you start cooking so that everything is ready to go and the spices don't burn.

PREPARE THE CHICKEN

6 skinless chicken breasts, each one cut into four large pieces (50g)

2 tsp ground turmeric

Put the chicken in a bowl, sprinkle over the turmeric and stir to coat. Cover the bowl with cling film and set aside in the fridge while you make the korma sauce.

COOK THE WHOLE SPICES

60ml vegetable oil

10 green cardamom pods

2 bay leaves

1–2 cloves

1 star anise

1 tbsp fennel seeds

Heat the oil in a large heavy-based saucepan over a medium heat. Add the cardamom, bay leaves, cloves, star anise and fennel seeds and cook for 1 minute, until fragrant.

MAKE THE KORMA SAUCE

2–3 large onions, sliced or chopped (500g)

1½ tsp fine sea salt

2 fresh green chillies, halved lengthways

60g fresh ginger, roughly chopped

4 garlic cloves, peeled and left whole

200g cashews (soaked ahead of time if you think of it)

200g thick Greek yoghurt

1 x 150g tin of tomato purée

200ml coconut milk

2 tsp ground cumin

2 tsp ground turmeric

pinch of ground mace or nutmeg

Add the onions and salt and cook for about 10 minutes, until softened and golden brown. Add the green chillies, ginger and garlic and cook for 2–3 minutes more, until fragrant.

Stir in the cashews (drained if you soaked them first), yoghurt, tomato purée, coconut milk, cumin, turmeric and mace or nutmeg. Add **500ml water**, then reduce the heat a little and simmer for 30 minutes, until the nuts are soft. Blend with a hand-held blender (including all the whole spices) until smooth.

Thin the sauce with another **150ml water** – the sauce should just coat the back of a spoon, almost like a custard. Add the chicken and simmer for about 20 minutes more, until the chicken is completely cooked through. You may need to partially cover the pan with a lid if the sauce is bubbling and splattering too much.

TO FINISH

50g butter

100ml cream

pinch of saffron

few drops of rosewater (optional)

Stir in the butter, cream, saffron and rosewater (if using). Remove the pan from the heat and allow the korma to settle for 5 minutes.

To serve Serve with plain boiled basmati rice (page 204) and warm naan (shop-bought or page 211).

SERVES **4** TO **6**

— MURGH CHETTIAR —
CHICKEN CHETTINAD
(A REAL MADRAS)

In India, Madras is a city, not a dish – and to make things even more confusing, Madras is now called Chennai – so when orders would come in for a chicken madras here in Ireland, I was never sure what it meant. Chettinad is a region south of Madras (Chennai), where the cuisine is known for the complexity of its flavours. This is the closest to an authentic chicken chettinad – a real madras – that you can make in Ireland. The squeeze of lemon juice at the end adds brightness, but if you can find tamarind pulp, use 2 tablespoons of that instead.

PREP

Measure out your spices into three separate small bowls: one bowl for all the spiced coconut powder ingredients; one for the red chilli and mustard seeds; and one for the paprika for the curry.

Prep and measure out all the remaining ingredients before you start cooking so that everything is ready to go and the spices don't burn.

MAKE THE SPICED COCONUT POWDER

- 100g desiccated coconut
- 1 tbsp cumin seeds
- 1 tbsp coriander seeds
- 1 tsp fennel seeds
- 1 tsp black peppercorns
- 3–4 star anise
- 3 fresh or dried red chillies, halved lengthways (or an extra 1½ tsp paprika added in step 3)

Toast the coconut, whole seeds, peppercorns, star anise and red chillies in a large, hot dry pan for 2–3 minutes, stirring. Allow to cool, then tip into a blender or food processor and grind to a powder. Set aside.

COOK THE WHOLE SPICES

- 50ml coconut or vegetable oil
- 1 fresh or dried red chilli, halved lengthways
- ½ tsp mustard seeds

Heat the oil in a large heavy-based saucepan over a medium heat. Add the red chilli and mustard seeds and cook for 1–2 minutes, until the mustard seeds start to pop.

3 MAKE THE CURRY

2 large red onions, finely diced

1½ tsp fine sea salt

1 tbsp grated or finely chopped fresh ginger

1 tbsp grated or finely chopped garlic

1½ tsp paprika

2 ripe tomatoes, roughly chopped

600g boneless, skinless chicken thighs or breasts, cut into large pieces (50g)

200ml coconut milk

squeeze of lemon juice

Add the onions and salt and cook for about 5 minutes, until softened. Add the ginger and garlic and cook for 1 minute more, stirring, until fragrant.

Add the spiced coconut powder, paprika and **50ml water**. Cook for 1 minute, stirring, then add the tomatoes. The mixture will be quite dry, almost like a paste. Add the chicken and stir to coat, then add another **200ml water** and simmer for 5 minutes. Stir in the coconut milk and lemon juice and simmer for 15–20 minutes more, until the chicken is completely cooked through.

4 TO FINISH

1 tbsp chopped fresh coriander

Stir in the chopped fresh coriander. Remove the pan from the heat and allow the curry to settle for 5 minutes.

To serve Garnish with shredded fresh basil and a few curry leaves (optional) and some grated coconut (if using), then serve with plain boiled basmati rice (page 204) and warm naan (shop-bought or page 211).

SERVES **4** TO **6**

— MURGH BIRYANI —
CHICKEN BIRYANI

Biryani is a festive dish. It's never made in small portions – it's a one-pot dish and the pot is big. Opening a pot of biryani is like a ceremony, especially if you use the traditional dough seal around the pot. Serve the rice gently with the back of the spoon so that you don't break it.

> **PREP**
>
> Measure out your spices into three separate small bowls: one bowl for the marinade spices; one for the bay leaves and salt for the rice; and one for the whole spices.
>
> Prep and measure out all the remaining ingredients before you start cooking so that everything is ready to go and the spices don't burn.

MARINATE THE CHICKEN

100g thick Greek yoghurt

50ml cream

juice of 1 small lime

1 heaped tbsp grated or finely chopped fresh ginger

1 heaped tbsp grated or finely chopped garlic

30g fresh mint, chopped

2 tbsp ground coriander

1½ tsp paprika

1 tsp ground cardamom

½ tsp ground mace or nutmeg

1 tbsp fine sea salt

25 whole black peppercorns

500g boneless, skinless chicken thighs or breasts, cut into large pieces (50g)

Whisk the yoghurt, cream, lime juice, ginger, garlic, mint, ground coriander, paprika, ground cardamom, mace or nutmeg, salt and peppercorns together in a large bowl, then add the chicken and stir to coat. Cover the bowl with cling film and marinate in the fridge for at least 30 minutes, but preferably 3–4 hours or overnight.

PARBOIL THE RICE

500g basmati rice

3 bay leaves

1½ tsp fine sea salt

Gently wash the rice in cold water at least three times, until the water runs clear, then leave to soak for 20–30 minutes (the longer you soak the rice, the less time it takes to cook). Bring a large saucepan filled with plenty of water to the boil with the bay leaves and salt, then reduce the heat and let it simmer for 15 minutes to allow the bay to infuse the water. Add the drained rice and bring the water back to the boil. Cook for only 5 minutes, stirring once or twice, then drain and set aside. You're just parboiling the rice here, so it will still be very firm and undercooked.

COOK THE WHOLE SPICES

80ml vegetable oil

6 green cardamom pods

2 star anise

2 bay leaves

1 cinnamon stick

1 tbsp cumin seeds

Meanwhile, heat the oil in a large heavy-based saucepan or casserole over a medium heat. Add the cardamom pods, star anise, bay leaves, cinnamon stick and cumin seeds and cook for 1 minute, until fragrant.

LAYER UP THE BIRYANI

1 large onion, thinly sliced (200g)

1 fresh green chilli, julienned

thumb-sized piece of fresh ginger, julienned

1 tbsp chopped fresh coriander

pinch of saffron

Add the onion and a pinch of salt and cook for about 10 minutes, until softened and golden brown. Add the marinated chicken, reduce the heat to low and cook for 10 minutes more. Once the oil has started to separate out at the edges of the pan, stir in **200ml water**.

Put the drained parboiled rice on top of the chicken in an even layer, but do not stir it in. Scatter over the green chilli, ginger, fresh coriander and saffron, but again, do not stir them in. The rice and spices should be left sitting on top of the chicken, undisturbed. Cover the pan with a tight-fitting lid (traditionally, we use a long snake of dough to seal the lid to the pot for a really tight fit) and simmer for 15 minutes more without lifting the lid. Once the cooking time is up, remove the pan from the heat and let it sit, still covered, for 10 minutes to settle.

TO FINISH

1 tbsp chopped fresh mint, plus extra to garnish

few drops of rosewater (optional)

Uncover the pan and gently stir to combine, then stir in the chopped fresh mint and rosewater (if using) just before serving.

To serve Garnish with a little more chopped fresh mint, then serve with a bowl of avocado, pomegranate and coriander raita (page 232) on the side to cool down the warming spices.

SERVES 4

— TANDOORI MURGH —
TANDOORI-STYLE CHICKEN

Before creating the recipe for this book I'd never once cooked this dish in an oven since I've always had access to a tandoor, so I was pleasantly surprised at how good it turned out. You won't get the same level of char on the chicken as you do when using a tandoor oven, which gets up to 500°C, but the chicken still has all the flavour of the traditional recipe. If you make a double batch, you can use the leftovers to make the chicken jalfrezi on page 46 the next day. Traditionally we'd use a whole jointed chicken, but if you use boneless, skinless chicken breasts, this will basically be a chicken tikka.

PREP

Measure out your spices into three separate small bowls: one bowl for the first marinade spices; one for the second marinade spices; and one for the paprika and salt for basting.

Prep and measure out all the remaining ingredients before you start cooking so that everything is ready to go.

PREPARE THE CHICKEN

2 part-boned chicken breasts, skin removed

2 chicken legs, bone in and skin removed

Make three or four deep incisions across each chicken portion, but don't cut all the way through.

MAKE THE FIRST MARINADE

juice of 1 lemon

1½ tsp grated or finely chopped fresh ginger

1½ tsp grated or finely chopped garlic

4 green cardamom pods, ground in a pestle and mortar (½ tsp ground)

2 tsp paprika

½ tsp ground mace or nutmeg

½ tsp garam masala

1 tsp fine sea salt

Mix all the ingredients for the first marinade together in a large bowl. Add the chicken to the marinade, stirring to coat. Cover the bowl with cling film and set aside for 20 minutes.

42 SPICE BOX

MAKE THE SECOND MARINADE

150g thick Greek yoghurt
50ml vegetable oil
½ tsp garam masala
½ tsp paprika
½ tsp fine sea salt
40ml cream

Mix together the yoghurt, oil, garam masala, paprika and salt in a separate bowl. It may look curdled at this point, but stir in the cream now to bring everything together. It should be very thick and smooth. Add to the chicken in the first marinade and stir to coat. Cover the bowl with cling film and marinate in the fridge for at least 30 minutes, but preferably 2–3 hours or overnight.

COOK THE CHICKEN

juice of ½ lime
1 tbsp melted butter
1 tbsp vegetable oil
½ tsp paprika
½ tsp fine sea salt

When you're ready to cook, preheat the oven to 220°C/200°C fan/gas 7. When I serve this dish I like to scrape up the juices and browned bits from the bottom of the baking tray, as that's where the best flavour is, and spoon them over the chicken. But for easier clean-up, you can line the tray with foil, then place a wire rack on top.

Mix together the lime juice, melted butter, oil, paprika and salt in a small bowl and set aside.

Put the marinated chicken on top of the wire rack on the baking tray. Cook in the preheated oven for 20 minutes, then remove the tray from the oven, baste the top of the chicken with the butter mixture and turn over. Baste again with the rest of the mixture, then return to the oven for another 20 minutes, until the chicken is completely cooked through.

To serve Garnish with a little chopped fresh coriander, then serve hot with plain boiled basmati rice (page 204), naan (shop-bought or page 211), pickled red onions (page 200) and mint and coriander chutney (page 224).

SERVES 4

— MURGH JALFREZI —
CHICKEN JALFREZI

In India jalfrezi is quite a dry dish, like a stir-fry, and it's always vegetarian – it might include cabbage, carrots, peppers or potatoes. But I've found that in Ireland people prefer it to be a little saucier and to include chicken, which is how I've made it here. If you use leftover tandoori-style chicken from the recipe on page 42 (or any other leftover cooked chicken), this will come together very quickly and you'll get a completely different dish.

> **PREP**
>
> Measure out your spices into three separate small bowls: one bowl for the whole spices; one for the coriander, paprika, turmeric and ground black pepper for the sauce; and one for the caster sugar.
>
> Prep and measure out all the remaining ingredients before you start cooking so that everything is ready to go and the spices don't burn.

COOK THE WHOLE SPICES

50ml vegetable oil

1 fresh or dried red chilli, halved lengthways

1 tsp cumin seeds

Heat the oil in a large heavy-based saucepan over a medium heat. Add the red chilli and cumin seeds and cook for 1 minute, until fragrant.

MAKE THE SAUCE

1 large red onion, finely diced

2 fresh green chillies, finely chopped

1 tsp fine sea salt

1 tbsp grated or finely chopped fresh ginger

1 tbsp grated or finely chopped garlic

1 tbsp ground coriander

1½ tsp paprika

¼ tsp ground turmeric

½ tsp freshly ground black pepper

1 x 227g tin of chopped tomatoes

1 tsp caster sugar

Add the diced red onion, green chillies and salt and cook for 5–8 minutes, until the onion has softened. Add the ginger and garlic and cook for 1 minute more.

Add the ground spices and **1 tablespoon of water** so that the spices don't burn. Cook for 1 minute, then add the tomatoes and sugar and simmer for 10 minutes to reduce the tomatoes a bit.

SPICE BOX

 ## STIR-FRY THE CHICKEN AND VEGETABLES

500g cooked chicken, roughly chopped (ideally leftover tandoori-style chicken from page 42)

2 peppers (any colour or a mix), thinly sliced

1 small red onion, thinly sliced

Add the chicken, peppers, sliced red onion and another **100ml water** to bring everything together. Cook, stirring, for 5 minutes – you want the peppers and onion to soften but still have some crunch.

 ## TO FINISH

1–2 tbsp chopped fresh coriander

Stir in the chopped fresh coriander. Remove the pan from the heat and allow the curry to settle for 5 minutes.

To serve *Serve with plain boiled basmati rice (page 204) and warm naan (shop-bought or page 211).*

SERVES **4**

— MURGH KHUBANI —
CHICKEN CURRY WITH DRIED APRICOTS

When I was doing my training in Mumbai in 1999 with the Oberoi Group, I became friends with another chef who was also training there. When I went to his house, his mother made this curry for us. I'd never had apricots and chicken together before. The apricots, cinnamon and cardamom make this quite a sweet curry. Caramel is traditionally added to this Parsi dish, which would make it even sweeter.

PREP

Measure out your spices into two separate small bowls: one bowl for the whole spices and one for the coriander, turmeric, paprika and cinnamon for the curry.

Prep and measure out all the remaining ingredients before you start cooking so that everything is ready to go and the spices don't burn.

SOAK THE APRICOTS

100g dried apricots

Put the dried apricots in a small bowl, cover with cold water and soak overnight (or for at least 30 minutes).

COOK THE WHOLE SPICES

50ml vegetable oil

3 green cardamom pods

1 cinnamon stick

Heat the oil in a large heavy-based saucepan over a medium heat. Add the cardamom pods and cinnamon stick and cook for 1 minute, until fragrant.

MAKE THE CURRY

1 large onion, thinly sliced

1½ tsp fine sea salt, plus extra to taste

3 fresh green chillies, halved lengthways (optional)

1 tbsp grated or finely chopped fresh ginger

5 garlic cloves, thinly sliced

1 tbsp ground coriander

1 tsp ground turmeric

1 tsp paprika

½ tsp ground cinnamon

4 skinless chicken breasts, cut into large pieces (50g)

1 large ripe tomato, chopped

pinch of saffron, soaked in 1 tbsp cream or milk

Add the onion and salt and cook for about 10 minutes, until softened. Add the green chillies (if using), ginger and garlic and cook for 1 minute more.

Add the coriander, turmeric, paprika, cinnamon and **50ml water** so that the spices don't burn. Cook for 1 minute, then add the chicken and tomato and cook for about 5 minutes, until the oil starts to separate out from the sauce around the edges of the pan.

Stir in the soaked and drained apricots and another **450ml water**. Simmer for 5 minutes, then stir in the saffron with the cream or milk it was soaked in and another ½ teaspoon of salt (or to taste). Cover, reduce the heat to low and simmer for 10–15 minutes, stirring occasionally but being careful not to mash the apricots. The chicken should be tender and completely cooked through.

TO FINISH

1 tbsp chopped fresh mint, plus extra small leaves to garnish

Stir in the chopped fresh mint, then remove the pan from the heat and allow the curry to settle for 5 minutes.

To serve Garnish with a few small fresh mint leaves, then serve with plain boiled basmati rice (page 204) and warm naan (shop-bought or page 211).

SERVES **4** TO **6**

— PALAK MURGH —
CHICKEN CURRY WITH SPINACH, HERBS AND CREAM

I created this recipe when I opened Tiffin in 2017 because I wanted to have something on the menu that was a little lighter and fresher. My version of this home-style curry is different from anyone else's because I add lots of fresh herbs in addition to the usual spinach (palak). I use watercress or rocket for pungency, basil for sweetness, coriander is always there and dill for its strong anise flavour.

PREP

Measure out the cumin, turmeric and paprika for the curry into a small bowl.

Prep and measure out all the remaining ingredients before you start cooking so that everything is ready to go and the spices don't burn.

1. MAKE THE CURRY

- 30g butter or ghee
- 2 tbsp vegetable oil
- 1 small red onion, finely diced (100g)
- 1½ tsp fine sea salt
- 2 fresh green chillies, halved lengthways
- thumb-sized piece of fresh ginger, chopped
- 4-5 garlic cloves, thinly sliced or chopped
- 1 tbsp ground cumin
- 1 tsp ground turmeric
- 1 tsp paprika
- 1 x 400g tin of chopped tomatoes (or 300g ripe tomatoes, chopped)
- 4 skinless chicken breasts, cut into large pieces (50g)

Heat the butter or ghee and the oil in a large heavy-based saucepan over a medium heat. Add the onion and salt and cook for about 5 minutes, until the onion is softened. Add the green chillies, ginger and garlic and cook for 1 minute more.

Add the cumin, turmeric, paprika and **50ml water** so that the spices don't burn, then stir in the tomatoes. Cook, covered, for about 5 minutes, until the tomatoes start to break down (if you're using fresh ones).

Add the chicken and another **200ml water**, then put the lid back on and simmer for 15-20 minutes, until the chicken is cooked through and tender.

2. TO FINISH

- 1 x 200g bag of baby spinach
- handful of watercress or rocket (optional)
- 20g fresh basil, chopped
- 10g fresh coriander, chopped
- 10g fresh dill, chopped
- 100ml cream or crème fraîche
- ½ tsp fine sea salt

Add the spinach, watercress or rocket (if using) and fresh herbs. The curry will be very thick with lots of vibrant green colour. Reduce the heat, then stir in the cream or crème fraîche and simmer gently for a few minutes, just until the spinach has wilted down. Adjust the seasoning with the ½ teaspoon of salt (or to taste). Remove the pan from the heat and allow the curry to settle for 5 minutes.

To serve *Serve with plain boiled basmati rice (page 204) and warm naan (shop-bought or page 211).*

CHAPTER 2

PORK, LAMB AND GOAT

SERVES 4

— ACHARI PASLIYAN —
PORK BELLY RIBS WITH COCONUT, MANGO AND STAR ANISE

My uncle used to make a sweet-and-sour version of these ribs with fresh mango and jaggery, which is a hard, golden brown type of cane sugar. (He wasn't really my uncle – in India, that's what we also call a close friend of the family.) I've adapted his recipe to make it quicker and using more commonly available ingredients, but if you want to make this even easier, you can use mango chutney straight from the jar without adding the extras that I've used here to boost the flavour. I guarantee that everyone will love these – in fact, it's my favourite recipe in the entire book.

PREP

Measure out the spices for the chutney glaze into a small bowl.

Prep and measure out all the remaining ingredients before you start cooking so that everything is ready to go and the spices don't burn.

BRAISE THE RIBS

1kg pork belly ribs, cut into portions

1 x 400ml tin of coconut milk

2 garlic cloves, peeled and left whole

thumb-sized piece of fresh ginger, sliced

4–5 star anise

2 tbsp tomato purée

1 tsp ground turmeric

1 tbsp fine sea salt

Put the ribs, coconut milk, garlic, ginger, star anise, tomato purée, turmeric, salt and **3 litres water** in a large pot and bring to the boil, then reduce the heat to low and simmer for 1 hour, until the ribs are cooked through. Remove the ribs from the pot and transfer to a baking tray. If you want to prep these ahead of time, you can chill the ribs in the fridge at this point.

MAKE THE CHUTNEY GLAZE

20ml vegetable oil

2 tbsp finely diced red onion

1 tsp paprika

½ tsp ground turmeric

¼ tsp nigella seeds

¼ tsp fine sea salt

1 tbsp white wine vinegar

100g shop-bought mango chutney

To make the mango chutney glaze, heat the oil in your largest frying pan over a medium heat. Add the onion, spices, salt, vinegar and **a splash of water** and cook for a few minutes, until the onion has softened. Add the mango chutney and stir to combine. Remove the pan from the heat and set aside.

SPICE BOX

DEEP-FRY OR OVEN BAKE THE RIBS

vegetable oil
(if deep-frying)

20g cornflour
(if deep-frying)

You can deep-fry the ribs or bake them in the oven, so either heat the oil in your deep-fryer to 190°C (or see the tips on page 19 if you don't have a deep-fryer) or preheat the oven to 240°C/220°C fan/gas 9 and line a baking tray with foil.

If deep-frying, toss the ribs in the cornflour. Working in batches, carefully add the ribs to the hot oil and fry for 3–4 minutes, until golden and crisp. Don't fry the ribs for too long or they'll start to dry out and toughen. Immediately transfer the ribs to the frying pan with the glaze and toss to coat.

If baking in the oven, transfer the ribs to the foil-lined baking tray and brush the mango chutney all over the ribs. Cook in the preheated oven for 15–20 minutes, until they are sticky, caramelised and just beginning to char a bit around the edges. Remove from the oven and allow to cool for a few minutes.

TO FINISH

fresh coriander leaves

½ small red onion, very finely diced

Pile the ribs on to a serving platter and scatter over the fresh coriander leaves and diced red onion to garnish.

MAKES **4**

— NARGISI KOFTA —
INDIAN-SPICED SCOTCH EGGS

In India these are called nargisi kofta, named after the legendary 1950s Bollywood star Nargis Dutt. When you cut the Scotch egg open lengthways, it was said to remind people of her beautiful big eyes. The lamb mixture is the same as for the lamb meatballs in the Goan meatball curry on page 68 but with extra spices, so if you want to make that curry too, make a double batch of the lamb mixture but leave out the fennel seeds and ground ginger in the batch you'll use for the curry.

PREP

Measure out your spices into three separate small bowls: one bowl for the spices for the Scotch eggs, one for the whole spices and one for the spices for the sauce.

Prep and measure out all the remaining ingredients before you start cooking so that everything is ready to go and the spices don't burn.

MAKE THE SCOTCH EGGS

Ingredients:

- 4 large free-range eggs
- 2–3 green cardamom pods
- 500g lamb mince – try to use mince with as little fat as possible
- 1 tbsp grated or finely chopped fresh ginger
- 1½ tsp grated or finely chopped garlic
- 1 tbsp chopped fresh mint
- 1 tbsp paprika
- 2 tsp ground cumin
- 1 tsp fennel seeds
- ½ tsp ground turmeric
- ½ tsp ground ginger
- 1½ tsp fine sea salt
- 80ml vegetable oil

Preheat the oven to 190°C/170°C fan/gas 5.

Place the eggs in a large saucepan of cold, salted water. Bring the water to the boil, then immediately reduce it to a simmer, lower in the eggs and cook for 8 minutes. Drain the water from the pan and run the eggs under cold water from the tap, then peel them and set aside. (You can boil the eggs ahead of time and keep them in the fridge, unpeeled.)

While the eggs are cooking, crush the cardamom pods in a pestle and mortar, then tip the powder into the small bowl with all the other Scotch egg spices.

Mix the lamb mince with the ginger, garlic, mint, spices and salt until well combined. The reason you should use mince with as little fat as possible is so that the mixture sticks together.

Divide the mince into four roughly equal portions. Flatten one portion into an oval shape in your hand, then place an egg on top. Wrap the mince around the egg, pinching it together at the seam, then smoothing the meat around the egg, making sure there are no gaps where the egg is peeking through. Don't be tempted to use too little meat per egg, as it shrinks when it cooks and a too-thin layer would pull away from the egg.

Heat the vegetable oil in a large frying pan over a medium-high heat. Add the Scotch eggs and sear until nicely browned all over, then transfer to a baking tray and cook in the preheated oven for 20–25 minutes.

COOK THE WHOLE SPICES

100ml vegetable oil

6 green cardamom pods

3–4 bay leaves

1 cinnamon stick

Meanwhile, heat the oil for the whole spices in a large heavy-based saucepan over a medium heat. Add the cardamom, bay leaves and cinnamon stick and cook for 1 minute, until fragrant.

MAKE THE SAUCE

2 medium onions, thinly sliced (250g)

1½ tsp fine sea salt

2 fresh green chillies, halved lengthways

1 tbsp grated or finely chopped fresh ginger

1 tbsp grated or finely chopped garlic

4 green cardamom pods, ground in a pestle and mortar (½ tsp ground)

2 tbsp ground coriander

1 tbsp paprika

1 tsp ground turmeric

¼ tsp ground mace or nutmeg

300g tomato passata

50g cashew butter

80ml cream

Add the onions and salt and cook for about 10 minutes, stirring occasionally, until softened and golden brown. Add the green chillies, ginger and garlic and cook for 1 minute.

Add the ground spices and **50ml water** so that the spices don't burn and cook for 1 minute. Stir in the passata, cashew butter and another **300ml water** and cook for a few minutes more. Use a hand-held blender to blitz the sauce (including the whole spices and bay leaves, though you could remove some or all of the chillies if you prefer) until it's smooth and thick. Stir in the cream (and **another splash of water** to thin the sauce a little more if needed). Add the Scotch eggs to the sauce and simmer for 5–10 minutes.

***To serve** Cut the eggs in half lengthways and spoon over the sauce. Serve with plain boiled basmati rice (page 204) on the side.*

SERVES 4 AS A LIGHT MEAL OR SNACK

— SHAMI KEBAB —
INDIAN LAMB PATTIES

These are traditionally made quite small – about 3cm in diameter – then deep-fried and served as a pre-dinner snack with a glass of whiskey or rum, which in India we drink before a meal instead of after it. We're pan-frying medium-sized patties here instead, but you could also make these into large patties and serve them as a burger in a toasted bun.

The cooking method for these patties is probably different from what you're used to. The mince and spices are simmered in water, then blended to a smooth paste before being formed into patties, which are quickly pan-fried just to give them a nice colour and crust.

PREP

Measure out your spices and herbs into two separate small bowls: one bowl for the whole spices, chillies and the cumin and fennel seeds for cooking the mince and one for the chopped fresh mint, paprika and garam masala to add to the mince later.

Prep and measure out all the remaining ingredients before you start cooking so that everything is ready to go and the spices don't burn.

SOAK THE LENTILS AND COOK THE MINCE

3 tbsp dried yellow split peas

100ml vegetable oil

6 black peppercorns

5 fresh or dried red chillies, halved lengthways

4 green cardamom pods

1 cinnamon stick

1 star anise

2 tsp cumin seeds

2 tsp fennel seeds

2 small red onions, finely diced

1½ tsp fine sea salt

3 garlic cloves, peeled and smashed

1 tbsp grated or finely chopped fresh ginger

700g lamb mince

Soak the yellow split peas in a small bowl of water for at least 30 minutes while you prep and measure out all your ingredients.

Heat the oil in a large heavy-based saucepan over a medium heat. Add the whole spices, chillies and the cumin and fennel seeds and cook for 1 minute, until fragrant. Add the onions and salt and cook for 5 minutes, until softened. Add the garlic and ginger and cook for 1 minute.

Drain the soaked lentils and add to the pan with the lamb mince stirring to combine and breaking up the mince with the back of the spoon. Stir in **200ml water** and bring to the boil, then cover the pan, reduce the heat and simmer for 30 minutes, until the yellow split peas are completely soft and the mince is cooked through. Uncover the pan and bring to the boil again. Continue to cook over a high heat, stirring occasionally, until all the liquid has evaporated but not to the point where the lamb is starting to catch and burn on the bottom of the pan.

Strain the mince through a fine-mesh sieve to drain off any remaining fat or liquid left in the pan – you need this mixture to be quite dry. Remove the red chillies, cinnamon stick and whole garlic cloves, then put the mince back in the pan and use a hand-held blender to blitz to a paste. It should be very dry, but again, this is what you want.

ADD TO THE COOKED MINCE

1 egg white, lightly beaten

2 tbsp cornflour

1 tbsp chopped fresh mint

1 tsp paprika

½ tsp garam masala

Stir in the egg white, cornflour, mint, paprika and garam masala until well combined. Set aside.

MAKE THE STUFFING

20g cashews, finely chopped

20g grated Cheddar cheese

1 fresh green chilli, finely chopped

1 tbsp chopped fresh mint

1 tsp grated or finely chopped fresh ginger

To make the stuffing, mix the cashews, Cheddar, chilli, mint and ginger in a small bowl.

Form the mince paste into medium-sized patties. Make an indent in the middle with your thumb and add 1 teaspoon of the stuffing, then form the meat around it to completely enclose the stuffing. Flatten the patties slightly.

COOK THE LAMB PATTIES

knob of butter or ghee

Melt the butter or ghee in a large frying pan over a high heat. Working in batches so that you don't crowd the pan, add the patties and cook for 2–3 minutes on each side, until nicely browned. Everything is already cooked, so you're just reheating them and forming a nice crust here.

To serve Serve warm with mint and coriander chutney (page 224) and apple and fennel salad (page 199) on the side.

SERVES **4**

— GOSHT KI CHAMPAIN —
TANDOORI LAMB CHOPS

We cook these lamb cutlets in the tandoor at my restaurants, but they would work brilliantly on the barbecue as a light summer dinner. I've suggested serving the chops with aloo chaat (potatoes with fresh herbs and pomegranate), but I also like to have this with a salad of rocket, goats' cheese, tomato, cooked beetroot and pomegranate seeds.

MARINATE THE LAMB CHOPS

1 small red onion, chopped

½ fennel bulb, sliced

thumb-sized piece of fresh ginger, chopped

1 tbsp paprika

2 tbsp malt vinegar

1 tbsp vegetable oil

1½ tsp fine sea salt

2 racks of lamb, cut into individual cutlets

Blitz the onion, fennel, ginger, paprika, vinegar, oil and salt together in a blender or food processor until smooth. Transfer to a large bowl.

Add the lamb cutlets and stir to coat. Cover the bowl with cling film and marinate in the fridge for at least 30 minutes, but preferably for a few hours or overnight.

MAKE THE SECOND MARINADE

80g thick Greek yoghurt

2 tbsp vegetable oil

1 tsp cayenne pepper

½ tsp fine sea salt

Mix all the ingredients for the second marinade together in a large bowl. Using a pastry brush, paint each side of the lamb cutlets with this second marinade, directly on top of the first marinade. Set aside for 30 minutes.

COOK THE CHOPS

2 tbsp vegetable oil

pinch of paprika

Heat the vegetable oil in a large frying pan over a high heat. Working in batches so that you don't crowd the pan, add the cutlets and cook for 45 seconds on each side just to sear them. Reduce the heat to medium and cook for 3 minutes more on each side for lamb that's cooked medium – it will still be a little pink inside (cook for a little longer if you like your lamb more well done). Sprinkle with a pinch of paprika to add a nice bit of colour.

To serve Serve with potatoes with fresh herbs and pomegranate (page 170 or see the intro) on the side.

SERVES 4 TO 6

— KEEMA KOFTA CURRY —
GOAN MEATBALL CURRY

We put this on the menu at Tiffin sometimes as a weekend special and it's always popular. We make our own lamb meatballs, but you could use ready-made plain beef meatballs from the butcher or supermarket to save time for a quick and easy midweek dinner. The Indian-spiced Scotch eggs on page 58 use this same meatball recipe with some extra spices, so if you want to make those too, make a double batch of this meatball mixture.

> **PREP**
>
> Measure out your spices into four separate small bowls: one bowl for the whole spices, one for the spices for the curry, one for the spices for the lamb meatballs and one for the garam masala to finish.
>
> Prep and measure out all the remaining ingredients before you start cooking so that everything is ready to go and the spices don't burn.

COOK THE WHOLE SPICES

120ml vegetable oil

4–5 green cardamom pods

1–2 bay leaves

1 tsp cumin seeds

Heat the oil in a large heavy-based saucepan over a medium heat. Add the cardamom, bay leaves and cumin seeds and cook for 1 minute, until fragrant.

MAKE THE CURRY

2 large red onions, finely diced

2 tsp fine sea salt

2 fresh green chillies, halved lengthways

2 tbsp grated or finely chopped fresh ginger

1 tbsp grated or finely chopped garlic

2 tbsp paprika

1 tbsp ground coriander

1 tsp ground turmeric

1 tsp freshly ground black pepper

½ tsp ground mace or nutmeg

400g tomato passata

Add the onions and salt and cook for about 5 minutes, stirring occasionally, until softened. Add the chillies, ginger and garlic and cook for 1 minute.

    Add the paprika, coriander, turmeric, ground black pepper and mace or nutmeg along with **50ml water** so that the spices don't burn. Cook for 1 minute, then stir in the passata and another **500ml water**. Bring to the boil, then reduce the heat to a simmer.

3 | MAKE THE MEATBALLS

500g lamb mince (try to use a mince with as little fat as possible)

1 tbsp grated or finely chopped fresh ginger

1½ tsp grated or finely chopped garlic

1 tbsp chopped fresh mint

8 green cardamom pods, ground in a pestle and mortar

1 tbsp paprika

2 tsp ground cumin

½ tsp ground turmeric

1 tsp fine sea salt

To make the meatballs, mix the lamb mince with the ginger, garlic, mint, spices and salt until well combined. The reason you should use mince with as little fat as possible is so that the meatballs stick together, otherwise they might fall apart when you poach them in the curry sauce.

Pinch off portions of the lamb mixture, roll into small balls (about the size of a golf ball) and add them directly to the sauce. Gently cook for 20 minutes over a low heat until the sauce has reduced and thickened slightly and the meatballs are cooked through.

4 | TO FINISH

120ml coconut milk

1 tbsp chopped fresh coriander, plus extra to garnish

½ tsp garam masala

Stir in the coconut milk, chopped fresh coriander and garam masala. Remove the pan from the heat and allow the curry to settle for 5 minutes.

To serve *Garnish with a little chopped fresh coriander, then serve on a bed of plain boiled basmati rice (page 204).*

SERVES **4** TO **6**

— KEEMA MATAR —
LAMB MINCE AND PEA CURRY

In India this is eaten more as a side dish and is never on the menu at restaurants, only street food vendors. One of my most frequent guests in a restaurant I worked at loved this curry. When I opened Pickle I didn't have it on my menu, but I would make it just for him. (I encouraged him to try the goat on toast on page 90 and now he loves that too.)

This is a mild curry that kids love. Adding whole pieces of green chilli means you add flavour without heat, as you can remove them before serving so that no one gets a big bite of chilli. But if you're worried that it might still be too spicy, just leave them out.

PREP

Measure out your spices into three separate small bowls: one bowl for the whole spices; one for the paprika, coriander, cumin and turmeric for the curry; and one for the garam masala to finish.

Prep and measure out all the remaining ingredients before you start cooking so that everything is ready to go and the spices don't burn.

COOK THE WHOLE SPICES

60ml vegetable oil

8 black peppercorns

4 cloves

3 bay leaves

2 or 3 green cardamom pods

1 cinnamon stick

Heat the oil in a large heavy-based saucepan over a medium heat. Add the peppercorns, cloves, bay leaves, cardamom pods and cinnamon stick and cook for 1 minute, until fragrant.

2   MAKE THE CURRY

2 medium red onions, finely diced (250g)

1 tbsp fine sea salt

2 fresh green chillies, halved lengthways (optional – see the intro)

2 tbsp grated or finely chopped fresh ginger

2 tbsp grated or finely chopped garlic

750g lamb mince

1 tbsp paprika

1 tbsp ground coriander

1½ tsp ground cumin

1 tsp ground turmeric

1 x 400g tin of chopped tomatoes

200g frozen peas

150g thick Greek yoghurt

Add the onions and salt and cook for about 5 minutes, stirring occasionally, until softened. Add the green chillies (if using), ginger and garlic and cook for 1 minute.

Add the lamb mince and mash it in really well with the back of a spoon. Cook for 5 minutes, until browned. Add the ground spices and **50ml water** so that the spices don't burn. Cook for 10 minutes, continuing to mash the mince until it's nice and smooth.

Add the tomatoes, peas, yoghurt and another **100ml water** and stir to combine. Simmer gently over a low heat for a few minutes to bring everything together.

3   TO FINISH

handful of shop-bought crispy onions

1 tbsp chopped fresh mint

1 tsp garam masala

Stir in the crispy onions, chopped fresh mint and garam masala. Remove the pan from the heat and allow the curry to settle for 5 minutes.

To serve *Serve with plain boiled basmati rice (page 204) and warm naan (shop-bought or page 211).*

SERVES **4** TO **6**

— DHANIWAL QORMA —
CREAMY LAMB KORMA WITH FRESH CORIANDER

This is a lovely fresh curry. Instead of using almond butter, you could use 70g of ground almonds and 2 tablespoons of water and mix it together to make a paste. Or you could omit the almond butter altogether, but it does add extra richness.

PREP

Measure out your spices into three separate small bowls: one bowl for the whole spices; one for the coriander, fennel seeds, ginger and saffron for the korma; and one for the ground fennel and ginger to finish.

Prep and measure out all the remaining ingredients before you start cooking so that everything is ready to go and the spices don't burn.

COOK THE WHOLE SPICES

80ml vegetable oil

4 star anise

2 cinnamon sticks

Heat the oil in a large heavy-based saucepan over a medium heat. Add the star anise and cinnamon sticks and cook for 1 minute, until fragrant.

MAKE THE KORMA

2 large onions, thinly sliced (300g)

1½ tsp fine sea salt

40g fresh ginger, chopped

1 tbsp finely chopped fresh green chilli

600g boneless diced leg of lamb

1½ tbsp ground coriander

1 tbsp fennel seeds, ground in a pestle and mortar

1 tsp ground ginger

pinch of saffron

150g thick Greek yoghurt

70g almond or cashew butter (or use 70g ground almonds mixed with 2 tbsp water)

Add the onions and salt and cook for about 10 minutes, stirring occasionally, until softened and golden brown. Add the ginger and green chilli and cook for 1 minute, stirring constantly.

Add the lamb and cook for a few minutes to brown, then add all the ground spices and saffron and cook for 1–2 minutes more. Add **500ml water**, stirring to scrape up any browned bits from the bottom of the pan. Bring to the boil, then reduce the heat, cover and simmer for 45–60 minutes, until the lamb is tender.

Whisk together the yoghurt and almond or cashew butter in a small bowl, then stir this into the curry along with another **500ml water**. Simmer for 15 minutes more. The sauce should be quite thin.

TO FINISH

100g fresh coriander

1 tbsp finely chopped fresh green chilli

1 tbsp chopped fresh mint

pinch of fennel seeds, ground in a pestle and mortar

pinch of ground ginger

½ tsp fine sea salt

You can either blend the coriander to a smooth purée with a little water or finely chop it. Either way, stir it into the curry just before serving along with the green chilli, mint, ground fennel and ground ginger, then adjust the seasoning with an extra ½ teaspoon of salt (or to taste). Remove the pan from the heat and allow the curry to settle for 5 minutes.

To serve *Scatter over one or two saffron threads and some flaked almonds. Drizzle with a little chilli oil and some mint and coriander chutney (page 224). Serve with plain boiled basmati rice (page 204) and warm naan (shop-bought or page 211).*

SERVES 4

— BENGALI BABU'S CHANA GOSHT —
SWEET POTATO AND CHICKPEA CURRY WITH RACK OF LAMB

In India sweet potatoes are white, not orange. My memories are of my mother roasting them over charcoal and eating them on their own, with butter, but I wanted to serve them in a more refined way. You could easily leave out the lamb altogether, in which case this would be a vegan curry. But lamb and chickpeas go together very well and sweet potatoes add a bit of sweetness. I learned this recipe from London chef Atul Kochhar when we cooked it together at the World Gourmet Summit in Singapore in 2013.

PREP

Measure out your spices into three separate small bowls: one bowl for the ground spices to marinate the lamb; one for the whole spices; and one for the coriander, paprika, cumin and turmeric for the curry.

Prep and measure out all the remaining ingredients before you start cooking so that everything is ready to go and the spices don't burn.

MARINATE THE LAMB

2 tbsp vegetable oil
1 tsp paprika
1 tsp ground coriander
½ tsp ground turmeric
½ tsp garam masala
1 tsp fine sea salt
2 racks of lamb

Mix together the oil, spices and salt for the marinade in a large bowl, then add the lamb racks, making sure they're well coated. Set aside to marinate for at least 30 minutes, but preferably for a few hours or overnight.

COOK THE SWEET POTATOES

500g sweet potatoes, peeled and cut into large pieces

Put the sweet potatoes in a pan, cover with cold water and bring to the boil. Reduce the heat and cook for about 10 minutes, until just cooked through but still holding their shape. Drain and set aside.

3 COOK THE WHOLE SPICES

100ml vegetable oil
1–2 cloves
1 bay leaf
2 tsp nigella seeds
1 tsp cumin seeds
1 tsp black peppercorns

Heat the oil in a large heavy-based saucepan over a medium heat. Add the cloves, bay leaf, nigella seeds, cumin seeds and peppercorns and cook for 1 minute, until fragrant.

4 MAKE THE CURRY

1 large red onion, finely diced (200g)
1½ tsp fine sea salt
1 tbsp grated or finely chopped fresh ginger
1 tbsp grated or finely chopped garlic
2 tbsp ground coriander
1 tbsp paprika
2 tsp ground cumin
1 tsp ground turmeric
2 x 400g tins of chickpeas, drained and rinsed
200g tomato passata

Add the onion and salt and cook for about 5 minutes, stirring occasionally, until softened. Add the ginger and garlic and cook for 1 minute.

Add the ground spices and **50ml water** so that the spices don't burn. Cook for 1 minute, then stir in the chickpeas, passata and another **200–300ml water**. Bring to the boil, then reduce the heat and simmer for about 15 minutes. Stir in the cooked sweet potatoes and cook for 5 minutes, until heated through.

5 COOK THE LAMB

1 tbsp vegetable oil

Meanwhile, preheat the oven to 220°C/200°C fan/gas 7.

Heat the oil in a large frying pan over a medium-high heat. Add the marinated lamb racks and cook for 1–2 minutes to sear on all sides, then transfer to a baking sheet and cook in the preheated oven for 15–20 minutes for pink, tender lamb (cook for a little longer if you like your lamb more well done). Leave to rest for 5 minutes, then cut the racks into individual cutlets.

6 TO FINISH

½ tsp fine sea salt
1 lemon wedge
1 tbsp chopped fresh coriander

Adjust the curry by seasoning with an extra ½ teaspoon of salt (or to taste) and a squeeze of lemon juice. Stir in the chopped fresh coriander, then remove the pan from the heat and allow the curry to settle for 5 minutes.

To serve Divide the curry between four wide, shallow bowls and add two or three lamb cutlets on top. Serve with plain boiled basmati rice (page 204) and warm naan (shop-bought or page 211).

SERVES **4** TO **6**

— ALOO GOSHT —
RAILWAY LAMB CURRY

This must be one of the most commonly used names for a lamb curry, but where does the name come from? In the golden era of train travel, if you had stayed at a guesthouse along the train line or if you were a first-class passenger on the train, this is what would be served. It's a traditional northern Indian dish, with large chunks of potatoes, onions and tomatoes to bulk out the lamb, which would have been expensive.

I have it on the menu at all my restaurants and one year I even served it at the Taste of Dublin food festival. We have a customer, Peter, who comes in every Sunday evening at half past eight without fail – so much so that if he's going to be out of the country or can't make it for some other reason, he'll tell us so that we don't worry. His favourite dish is this railway lamb curry.

> **PREP**
>
> Measure out your spices into three separate small bowls: one bowl for the whole spices; one for the coriander, paprika and turmeric for the curry; and one for the garam masala to finish.
>
> Prep and measure out all the remaining ingredients before you start cooking so that everything is ready to go and the spices don't burn.

COOK THE WHOLE SPICES

100ml vegetable oil

8 cloves

6 green cardamom pods

2 star anise

1 cinnamon stick

1½ tsp cumin seeds

1 tsp black peppercorns

Heat the oil in a large heavy-based saucepan over a medium heat. Add the cloves, cardamom pods, star anise, cinnamon stick, cumin seeds and peppercorns and cook for 1 minute, until fragrant.

2. MAKE THE CURRY

2 large onions, thinly sliced (350g)

1½ tsp fine sea salt

2 fresh green chillies, halved lengthways

1 tbsp grated or finely chopped ginger

1 tbsp grated or finely chopped garlic

2 tbsp ground coriander

2 tbsp paprika

1 tsp ground turmeric

1kg boneless diced leg of lamb

500g baby potatoes, halved or quartered

200g tomato passata or 1 x 227g tin of chopped tomatoes

handful of cherry tomatoes (optional)

Add the onions and salt and cook for about 10 minutes, stirring occasionally, until softened and golden brown. Add the chillies, ginger and garlic and cook for 1 minute.

Add the ground spices and **50ml water** so that the spices don't burn. Cook for 1 minute. Add the lamb and stir to coat, then pour in another **100ml water** and cook for a few minutes more. Add **1 litre water** and bring to the boil, then cover the pan, reduce the heat and simmer for 1½ hours, stirring occasionally.

Stir in the potatoes, passata and cherry tomatoes (if using), then cover and cook for 30 minutes more, until the potatoes are cooked through and the lamb is tender.

3. TO FINISH

1 tbsp chopped fresh coriander, plus extra to garnish

1 tsp garam masala

Stir in the chopped fresh coriander and garam masala. Remove the pan from the heat and allow the curry to settle for 5 minutes.

To serve *Garnish with a little chopped fresh coriander and shredded fresh mint, then serve with plain boiled basmati rice (page 204) and warm naan (shop-bought or page 211).*

SERVES 4

— CHHA GOSHT —
LAMB CURRY WITH HIMALAYAN SPICES

Chha means buttermilk, which is what this dish would traditionally be made with, but I've used yoghurt instead to cut through the richness of the lamb. Back in India, I once worked for a chef who also worked for the royal family and he showed us how to make this dish. It's simple yet it's something of a special occasion dish that's often served at buffets. Sometimes dried mango is added to it. This is a mild curry that's very popular in my Street takeaway, where we call it shimla gosht (named after Shimla, the capital city of the northern Indian state of Himachal Pradesh). I wanted to do something different, and when people ask me what they should try, I always suggest this.

PREP

Measure out your spices into two separate small bowls: one bowl for the whole spices and one for the coriander, turmeric and paprika for the curry.

Prep and measure out all the remaining ingredients before you start cooking so that everything is ready to go and the spices don't burn.

1. COOK THE WHOLE SPICES

- 80ml vegetable oil
- 2 bay leaves
- 2 fresh or dried red chillies, halved lengthways
- 1 cinnamon stick
- 1½ tsp coriander seeds
- 1 tsp cumin seeds
- 1 tsp mustard seeds

Heat the oil in a large heavy-based saucepan over a medium heat. Add the bay leaves, red chillies, cinnamon stick and seeds and cook for 1 minute, until fragrant.

MAKE THE CURRY

1 small red onion, thinly sliced (100g)

1½ tsp fine sea salt

2 fresh green chillies, halved lengthways

3 garlic cloves, peeled and smashed

1 tbsp chopped fresh ginger

2 tbsp ground coriander

1½ tsp ground turmeric

1½ tsp paprika

30g rice flour or gram flour (optional)

600g boneless diced leg of lamb

500g thick Greek yoghurt

Add the onions, green chillies and salt and cook for about 10 minutes, stirring occasionally, until softened and golden brown. Add the garlic and ginger and cook for 1 minute, stirring constantly.

Add the ground spices and **50ml water** so that the spices don't burn. Cook for 1 minute, then sprinkle in the flour (if using) and stir until smooth – you don't want there to be any lumps at this point. Add the lamb and stir to coat it in the spice paste, then increase the heat to high and cook for a few minutes to brown.

In a separate bowl, whisk together the yoghurt and **800ml water**, then pour this into the pan and stir to combine. Bring to the boil, then reduce the heat, cover and simmer for at least 1½ hours, until the lamb is tender. Stir occasionally and add **a splash of water** if the curry is sticking to the bottom of the pan, which it might do if you've used the flour.

TO FINISH

large handful of baby spinach leaves

1 tbsp chopped fresh coriander

Just before serving, stir in the spinach and chopped fresh coriander and allow the spinach to wilt. Remove the pan from the heat and allow the curry to settle for 5 minutes.

To serve Serve with plain boiled basmati rice (page 204) and warm naan (shop-bought or page 211).

SERVES **4**

— NALLI KI KALIYA —
LAMB SHANKS WITH TOMATOES, ALMONDS AND YOGHURT

I started making this back in the early 2000s, when no one was serving lamb shanks in Indian restaurants here, but it quickly became a popular dish. I prefer goat shanks, which is what we always use in India. Goat shanks are smaller than lamb shanks and much more flavoursome, but either type works.

Traditionally you'd use double the number of spices that I've used here, but I've streamlined it to make it more suitable to make at home. A few drops of rosewater added at the very end along with the lemon is lovely if you can source it.

As a make-ahead option, you could put all the ingredients from steps 1 and 2 (except the passata and almonds) in a heavy-based casserole, mix it all together and chill overnight. The next day, add the litre of water (or enough to cover), cover with a lid and cook it in the oven at 220°C/200°C fan/gas 7 for 10 minutes, then reduce the heat to 180°C/160°C fan/gas 4 and cook for 2–3 hours, until the meat is tender. Remove the shanks and blend the sauce.

PREP

Measure out your spices into two separate small bowls: one bowl for the whole spices and one for the coriander, paprika, turmeric and mace or nutmeg for the lamb shanks.

Prep and measure out all the remaining ingredients before you start cooking so that everything is ready to go and the spices don't burn.

COOK THE WHOLE SPICES

100ml vegetable oil

6-8 green cardamom pods

5 cloves

2 cinnamon sticks

2 bay leaves

1-2 fresh or dried red chillies, halved lengthways

1 tsp cumin seeds

1 tsp black peppercorns

Heat the oil in a large heavy-based saucepan or casserole over a medium heat. Add the cardamom, cloves, cinnamon, bay leaves, red chillies, cumin seeds and peppercorns and cook for 1 minute, until fragrant.

COOK THE LAMB SHANKS

2 red onions, thinly sliced

1 tbsp fine sea salt

3 fresh green chillies, halved lengthways

2 tbsp grated or finely chopped fresh ginger

2 tbsp grated or finely chopped garlic

4 lamb or goat shanks

3 tbsp ground coriander

1½ tbsp paprika

1 tsp ground turmeric

¼ tsp ground mace or nutmeg

100g thick Greek yoghurt

200g tomato passata

60g ground almonds

Add the onions and salt and cook for about 10 minutes, stirring occasionally, until softened and golden. Add the green chillies, ginger and garlic and cook for 1 minute.

Working in batches if necessary so that you don't crowd the pan, add the lamb or goat shanks and brown them all over, then add the ground spices (you really do need 3 tablespoons of ground coriander to stand up to the strong flavour of the lamb here, that isn't a mistake!) and **50ml water** so that the spices don't burn.

Whisk the yoghurt with another **50ml water** in a small bowl or jug, then add to the pan along with the passata, ground almonds and **1 litre water** (or enough water to completely cover the shanks). Cover the pan and bring to the boil, then reduce the heat and simmer for 2–3 hours, until the meat is tender and easily pulls away from the bone.

TO FINISH

1 lemon wedge

1 tbsp chopped fresh coriander

Transfer the lamb shanks to a plate, then blend the sauce (including all the whole spices) with a hand-held blender until smooth. Finish with a squeeze of lemon juice.

Serve one lamb shank per person in a wide, shallow bowl with plenty of the sauce spooned around, then scatter over the chopped fresh coriander.

To serve Serve with plain boiled basmati rice (page 204) and warm naan (shop-bought or page 211).

SERVES **6** TO **8**

— LUCKNOWI RAAN —
BRAISED LAMB WITH WHOLE SPICES

We call this our lamb raan feast in Pickle and it needs to be ordered 48 hours in advance. For the past couple of years, we've offered it as a Christmas Eve and New Year's Eve treat. You get a whole leg of lamb plus black lentils, saffron sauce, cumin pulao, raita, mint and coriander chutney and plenty of warm butter naan.

In the Bukhara restaurant in the luxury ITC Maurya hotel in Delhi – widely considered to be one of the best restaurants not just in India, but in all of Asia – the menu hasn't changed since they opened in 1978 because the food is so well loved and so consistent. If you have something there and go back five years later, it will still taste the same. This is one of the dishes they serve. It's a traditional recipe from the nawabs (the upper class or nobility) of the city of Lucknow. It's a great dish for a family get-together or celebration.

PREP

Measure out your spices into three separate small bowls: one bowl for the marinade spices; one for the whole spices; and one for the paprika, turmeric, nutmeg and saffron for braising.

Prep and measure out all the remaining ingredients before you start cooking so that everything is ready to go and the spices don't burn.

PREPARE THE LAMB

1 x 1.5kg leg of lamb

Trim off any extra fat from the lamb, then cut some nice deep gashes on the top.

MARINATE THE LAMB

100g thick Greek yoghurt

juice of 1 lemon

50g cashews, toasted and crushed

10g fresh mint, chopped

1 tbsp grated or finely chopped fresh ginger

1 tbsp grated or finely chopped garlic

2 tbsp paprika

2 tbsp ground coriander

1 tbsp fine sea salt

1 tsp ground turmeric

Mix all the marinade ingredients together, then rub it on the lamb. Cover the lamb loosely with cling film and marinate it for as long as possible – preferably overnight, but even just 30 minutes will do.

COOK THE WHOLE SPICES

2 tbsp butter or ghee

8 green cardamom pods

4 cloves

3 bay leaves

2 star anise

1 cinnamon stick

15–20 black peppercorns

Preheat the oven to 220°C/200°C fan/gas 7.

Melt the butter or ghee in a heavy-based casserole over a medium heat. Add the cardamom, cloves, bay leaves, star anise, cinnamon stick and peppercorns and cook for 1 minute, until fragrant.

COOK THE LAMB

200g sliced shallots

1 tsp fine sea salt

2 fresh green chillies, halved lengthways

1 tbsp roughly chopped fresh ginger

1 tbsp paprika

½ tsp ground turmeric

½ tsp grated nutmeg

pinch of saffron

40g tomato purée

1.5 litres lamb stock or water

Add the shallots and salt and cook for about 5 minutes, until softened. Add the green chillies, ginger, paprika, turmeric, nutmeg and saffron and cook for 1 minute, then stir in the tomato purée and **50ml water**.

Put the leg of lamb in a roasting tin, then scrape in the shallot mixture and roast in the preheated oven for 10–12 minutes.

Remove the tin from the oven, pour in the lamb stock or water and cover the tin tightly with foil. Reduce the oven temperature to 180°C/160°C fan/gas 4 and return the lamb to the oven to roast for 1 hour 20 minutes–1 hour 30 minutes for lamb that is nice and pink (or cook it for longer, until the lamb is done to your liking).

Remove the lamb from the roasting tin to a serving platter and loosely cover with foil to rest. Pour all the juices, whole spices and shallots from the tin into a blender and blitz together, then pour into a clean saucepan through a fine-mesh sieve. Bring to the boil, then lower the heat a bit and simmer vigorously until the sauce has reduced and thickened. Taste it and check the seasoning, then pour into a serving bowl.

To serve *Scatter a little shredded fresh mint over the leg of lamb, then take it to be carved into slices at the table. Serve with spiced basmati rice with peas and red onion (page 208), pickled cucumber and red onion raita (page 230), mint and coriander chutney (page 224), warm naan (shop-bought or page 211), 4 ripe sliced tomatoes and pickled red onions (page 200) for a feast.*

SERVES **4** TO **6**

— KEEMA PAO —
GOAT ON TOAST

I put this on the menu when we opened Pickle in 2016 and it's become one of my signature dishes. Essentially, it's a goat mince curry served with brioche instead of the usual rice.

When I arrived in Ireland I was surprised to see that goat meat wasn't readily available, even though you could easily get goats' milk and cheese. But I was determined to put it on my menu at Pickle. It was hard to convince people to try it when we opened, so I said that if they didn't like it, they could send it back and I'd give them something else. But not one person has ever sent it back.

These days we can source Irish goat from producers such as Broughgammon Farm in County Antrim, Ballinwillin House Farm in County Cork and Irish Goat Meat in County Roscommon. But if you can't get goat mince, use lamb mince instead.

PREP

Measure out your spices into two separate small bowls: one bowl for the whole spices and one for the coriander, cumin, paprika, turmeric and garam masala for the sauce.

Prep and measure out all the remaining ingredients before you start cooking so that everything is ready to go and the spices don't burn.

PREPARE THE MINCE

800g–1kg lean goat or lamb mince

Before you start to cook, put the mince in a large bowl and add **a splash of water**. Use your hands to mix into a smooth paste, then set aside.

COOK THE WHOLE SPICES

80ml vegetable oil

6 green cardamom pods

4 bay leaves

3 cloves

2 cinnamon sticks

Heat the oil in a large heavy-based saucepan over a medium heat. Add the cardamom, bay leaves, cloves and cinnamon sticks and cook for 1 minute, until fragrant.

3. MAKE THE SAUCE

400g finely chopped banana shallots

1½ tsp fine sea salt

1 fresh green chilli, finely chopped

1 tbsp grated or finely chopped fresh ginger

1 tbsp grated or finely chopped garlic

2 tbsp ground coriander

1 tbsp ground cumin

1 tbsp paprika

1 tsp ground turmeric

1 tsp garam masala

1 x 400g tin of chopped tomatoes

250g thick Greek yoghurt

Add the shallots and salt and cook for 2 minutes, stirring occasionally, until soft. Add the green chilli, ginger and garlic and cook for 1 minute more.

Stir in the ground spices and **50ml water** so that the spices don't burn. Cook for 1 minute – the mixture will be very thick. Add the mince and increase the heat to high. Cook for 5 minutes, stirring constantly so that nothing catches on the bottom of the pan.

Stir in the tomatoes, yoghurt and another **100ml water**. Reduce the heat to low and continue to cook for 30–35 minutes, stirring occasionally, until the mince is completely cooked through. If it looks too dry, add a little more water.

4. TO FINISH

1 tbsp chopped fresh coriander

1 tbsp chopped fresh mint

Divide the curry between shallow serving bowls and scatter over some chopped fresh coriander and mint.

To serve Serve with 4–6 thick slices of toasted brioche, lime wedges and some very finely diced red onion on the side.

PORK, LAMB AND GOAT

CHAPTER 3

★

SEAFOOD

SERVES **4** AS A SNACK OR SIDE

— KARWARI JHINGA —
CRISPY PRAWNS WITH DILL RAITA

This dish is a perfect example of what we call chakhna in India – small bites of food that you eat over a few beers with friends. It brings me back to my teenage years back home. Karwar is a city at the mouth of the Kali River on the west coast of southern India with a strong fishing community, so they have a rich repertoire of seafood recipes such as this one. You can also make this with cod strips, which kids love.

PREP

Prep and measure out all the spices and ingredients before you start cooking so that everything is ready to go.

MAKE THE BATTER

3 tbsp cornflour

2 tbsp plain flour

2 tsp paprika

1 tsp nigella seeds

1 tsp fennel seeds

1 tsp fine sea salt

5g chopped fresh dill, plus extra to garnish

600g cleaned and deveined frozen black

Mix together the flours, paprika, nigella seeds, fennel seeds, salt and dill in a large bowl, then add the prawns and gently toss to coat. Add **40ml water** and toss again until the prawns are very lightly coated in the batter. The prawns are only meant to have a light dusting of flour and spices, not be coated in a thick batter.

COOK THE PRAWNS

vegetable oil, for deep-frying

Heat the oil in a deep-fryer to 180°C (or see the tips on page 19 if you don't have a deep-fryer).

Working in batches, carefully add the prawns to the hot oil and deep-fry for 2–3 minutes, until cooked through and crisp. Transfer to a plate lined with kitchen paper to absorb the excess oil. Repeat until all the prawns are cooked.

To serve *Garnish with a little fresh dill and some grated coconut (optional). Serve the crispy prawns with a lime wedge for squeezing over and a small bowl of dill raita (page 228) on the side for dipping.*

SPICE BOX

SERVES 4

— TANDOORI JHINGA —
JUMBO PRAWNS WITH MANGO AND AVOCADO SALAD

Everyone loves prawns – we go through 25 kilograms of peeled and deveined prawns in a week at Pickle. These prawns are perfect for the barbecue, as keeping them in the shell stops the delicate meat from burning or overcooking, but they also work well cooked on a griddle pan on the hob. Keeping the shell on also improves the flavour and reduces the need for salt, as the shell naturally adds some briny flavour.

PREP

Prep and measure out all the ingredients before you start cooking so that everything is ready to go and the spices don't burn.

MAKE THE SALAD DRESSING

50ml rapeseed oil

zest and juice of ½ lime

1 tsp balsamic vinegar

1 tsp fish sauce

½ tsp chilli flakes

½ tsp caster sugar

½ tsp fine sea salt

Start by whisking together all the salad dressing ingredients.

MAKE THE MANGO AND AVOCADO SALAD

1 ripe mango, peeled and diced

1 ripe avocado, peeled, stoned and diced

40g rocket

handful of fresh coriander leaves

20g pumpkin seeds, toasted

Put the mango, avocado, rocket and coriander leaves in a large bowl, then drizzle over the dressing and toss gently to coat. Finish with the toasted pumpkin seeds and set aside.

COOK THE PRAWNS

16 raw jumbo prawns, unpeeled and butterflied

zest and juice of 1 lime

2-3 dried lime leaves

thumb-sized piece of fresh ginger, grated

1 tbsp paprika

1 tsp fine sea salt

2 tbsp vegetable oil

2 tbsp coconut milk, for basting

1 tbsp chopped fresh coriander

To butterfly the prawns for this recipe, cut them in half lengthways from top to tail but without cutting all the way through the shell, then press them out flat.

Heat up a griddle pan over a high heat on the hob (it's fine to use a regular frying pan if you don't have a griddle pan).

Put the prawns, lime zest, lime leaves, grated ginger, paprika, salt and oil in a large bowl and toss to coat.

Add the prawns to the hot pan, butterflied side down. Cook for 60–90 seconds on each side, then use a pastry brush to baste the prawns all over with the coconut milk and squeeze in the lime juice. Cook for 1–2 minutes more if necessary, just until the prawns are cooked through – the shell should be pink and the meat should be white and firm, but not tough or rubbery. Add the chopped fresh coriander at the very end.

To serve *Divide the mango and avocado salad between four plates, then add four prawns to each plate and spoon over the sauce from the pan.*

SERVES **4** TO **6**

— SAMUNDARI KHAZANA —
GOAN-STYLE MIXED SEAFOOD CURRY

This is an easy recipe using common spices, but the secret is to use them in the right way and in the right quantity. At Pickle I'm committed to serving food from northern India, but I love this curry so much that I reinvented a traditional Goan seafood curry to use the spices that I always have in my spice box. (Seafood isn't as commonly eaten in northern India as it is in parts of the country that are near the coast.) The point is that once you understand how to use spices, you can take any recipe and use it as a springboard to create your own. I've used a mix of shellfish here, but the main thing is to use around 1kg of shellfish in total.

> **PREP**
>
> Measure out your spices into three separate small bowls: one bowl for the toasted spice mix; one for the whole spices; and one for the paprika and turmeric for the curry.
>
> Prep and measure out all the remaining ingredients before you start cooking so that everything is ready to go and the spices don't burn.

MAKE THE TOASTED SPICE MIX

2 tbsp coriander seeds

1 tbsp cumin seeds

3 green cardamom pods

1 fresh or dried red chilli, halved lengthways

1 clove

1 cinnamon stick

Toast the coriander and cumin seeds, cardamom pods, red chillies, clove and cinnamon stick in a large hot, dry pan over a medium-high heat for a few minutes until fragrant. Stir or shake the pan occasionally to ensure the spices toast evenly. Tip out on to a plate and allow to cool completely before blitzing to a fine powder in a coffee grinder or NutriBullet blender. You need to blend the toasted spices on their own in this step, so don't be tempted to skip it. If you added the toasted dry spices to the curry later on without blending them first here, they wouldn't blend properly because the sauce is too wet and you'd never get a smooth purée.

② COOK THE WHOLE SPICES

60ml vegetable oil

4-5 green cardamom pods

1 fresh or dried red chilli, halved lengthways

1 clove

1 cinnamon stick

Heat the oil in a large heavy-based saucepan over a medium-low heat. Add the cardamom, red chilli, clove and cinnamon stick and cook for 1 minute, until fragrant.

③ MAKE THE CURRY

2 onions, sliced

1½ tsp fine sea salt

thumb-sized piece of fresh ginger, chopped

4-5 large garlic cloves, chopped

1 tbsp paprika

1½ tsp ground turmeric

100g tomato purée

1½ x 400ml tins of coconut milk

50ml apple cider vinegar

4-6 Dublin Bay prawns, shell on

250g mussels

250g cockles

250g clams

250g peeled prawns

250g pre-cooked crab claws (optional)

Add the onions and salt and cook for about 10 minutes, stirring occasionally, until softened but not browned. Add the ginger and garlic and cook for 1 minute, then add the paprika, turmeric and **50ml water**. Reduce the heat to low and cook for 1 minute, then add 4 tablespoons of the toasted spice mix and another **50ml water** and simmer for a few minutes to bring everything together to form the base of the curry. It will be very thick at this point.

Add the tomato purée, coconut milk, apple cider vinegar and another **300ml water**. Raise the heat back up to medium, simmer and allow to reduce a bit while you cook the shellfish.

Clean the mussels by pulling off any barnacles or beards, then rinse the mussels, cockles and clams in several changes of cold water. Make sure each and every cockle, mussel and clam is tightly shut. If any are even slightly open, tap it on the counter – if it closes within a few seconds, it's safe to eat. If it doesn't it means it's dead, so throw it out.

Bring **350ml water** to the boil in a large stockpot, then tip in the whole Dublin Bay prawns, cockles, mussels and clams. Cover the pot with a tight-fitting lid and reduce the heat to medium. Steam for 3–5 minutes, stirring or shaking the pot once or twice, until they have all opened up. Discard any that remain closed. Drain.

Blend the slightly reduced sauce (including all the whole spices) with a hand-held blender until smooth and thick, then stir in the cooked mussels, cockles and clams along with the prawns and crab claws (if using). Simmer for a few minutes, just until the prawns are cooked and the crab claws are heated through. Remove the pan from the heat and allow the curry to settle for 5 minutes.

To serve Serve with plain boiled basmati rice (page 204).

SERVES 4

— MEEN MOILEE —
COCONUT FISH CURRY

This recipe comes from Kerala, a state on the tropical Malabar Coast in south-western India. I've used just one green chilli here but I sometimes add as many as six – you're using them for flavour, not heat, as they are removed at the end. Add as many as you like depending on how spicy your chillies are and your own preference for heat. If you have access to an Asian or Indian market, try adding 20 curry leaves along with the coconut milk for extra depth of flavour.

PREP

Measure out your spices into three separate bowls: one medium bowl for the turmeric and salt for the fish; one small bowl for the cardamom pods and salt for cooking the onions; and one small bowl for the ground coriander and turmeric.

Prep and measure out all the remaining ingredients before you start cooking so that everything is ready to go and the spices don't burn.

1 MAKE THE CURRY

2 tbsp coconut oil

2 medium red onions, finely diced

3 garlic cloves, thinly sliced

1 fresh red chilli, halved lengthways

1 fresh green chilli, halved lengthways

3 green cardamom pods

½ tsp fine sea salt

1½ tsp ground coriander

½ tsp ground turmeric

1 x 400ml tin of coconut milk

125g cherry tomatoes

Melt the coconut oil in a large saucepan over a medium heat. Add the onions, garlic, red and green chillies, cardamom pods and salt and cook for 5 minutes, until the onions are softened and translucent.

Add the ground coriander, turmeric and **50ml water** so that the spices don't burn. Cook for 1 minute, then pour in the coconut milk and bring to a simmer. Cook for a few minutes to let the coconut milk reduce and thicken slightly, then stir in another **120ml water**.

Add the spiced fish fillets, pushing them down into the coconut milk, along with the whole cherry tomatoes. Simmer gently for about 5 minutes while you cook the fish.

2 COOK THE FISH

1 tsp ground turmeric

1 tsp fine sea salt

4 x 150g sea bass or sea bream fillets, skin on and deboned

1 tbsp vegetable oil

knob of butter

Mix the turmeric and salt together in a medium bowl, add the fish and toss gently with a rubber spatula to coat (otherwise the turmeric will stain your hands and nails yellow).

Heat the oil in a large non-stick frying pan over a medium-high heat. Make sure the pan is nice and hot before you add the fish fillets, skin side down. Press each fillet down gently with a spatula for a few seconds, then let them cook without touching them for 2–3 minutes so than the skin gets really crisp. Flip the fish over, add the butter to the pan and cook for 2 minutes more, until the fish is cooked through.

3 TO FINISH

1 tbsp chopped fresh coriander

Stir in the chopped fresh coriander, then remove the pan from the heat and allow the curry to settle for 5 minutes. Divide the curry between four bowls and add a fish fillet to each one, skin side up.

To serve Serve with plain boiled basmati rice (page 204).

MAKES **8**

— MACHHI KI TIKKI —
FISH CAKES WITH MASALA MAYO

When I was opening a restaurant in 2005, Indian-spiced fish wasn't being served anywhere. We wanted to create a dish that everyone would love, so we came up with these fish cakes. They were so popular that we put them on the menus of the entire restaurant group – they were still on the menu when I left the group 14 years later.

These fish cakes are a fusion of Indian and Thai food and are the perfect way to use up leftover cooked fish. I usually use cod, salmon or even stone bass, but any fish will work. I don't like to use fresh fish for fish cakes because I find the texture to be too bouncy, but if you're making these from scratch, start with 500g fresh, uncooked fish and cook it on a baking tray in the oven at 220°C/200°C fan/gas 7 for about 15 minutes, until cooked through.

> **PREP**
>
> Measure out your spices into two separate small bowls: one bowl for the paprika, fennel, turmeric and salt for the masala mayo and one for the fennel seeds, nigella seeds and turmeric for the fish cakes.
>
> Prep and measure out all the remaining ingredients before you start cooking so that everything is ready to go and the spices don't burn.

MAKE THE PICKLE

1 cucumber, peeled, deseeded and thinly sliced

1 small red onion, thinly sliced

6 stems of fresh dill, roughly torn

4 tbsp white wine vinegar

2 tsp grated or finely chopped fresh ginger

1 tsp fine sea salt

Mix together the cucumber, red onion, dill, vinegar, ginger and salt in a small bowl and set aside for 30 minutes to lightly pickle while you make the fish cakes, then drain.

COOK THE POTATOES

500g Rooster or Maris Piper potatoes, peeled

Cook the whole peeled potatoes in a saucepan of boiling salted water until cooked through but still holding their shape. Drain and set aside to cool, then grate using the large holes on a box grater.

MAKE THE MASALA MAYO

1 tbsp vegetable oil

1 fresh green chilli, finely chopped

¼ fresh red chilli, finely chopped

1 tbsp grated or finely chopped fresh ginger

1 tsp paprika

½ tsp fennel seeds, ground in a pestle and mortar

pinch of ground turmeric

¼ tsp fine sea salt

squeeze of lemon juice

2 tbsp mayonnaise

Meanwhile, make the masala mayo. Heat the oil in a small frying pan over a medium heat, then remove the pan from the heat. Add the green and red chillies, ginger, ground spices, salt and a squeeze of lemon, then transfer to a bowl and allow to cool before stirring in the mayonnaise until well combined. Chill in the fridge while you finish making the fish cakes.

COOK THE FISH CAKES

1 tbsp vegetable oil, plus extra for frying

1 tbsp grated or finely chopped fresh ginger

1½ tsp grated or finely chopped garlic

1½ tsp fennel seeds

½ tsp nigella seeds

¼ tsp ground turmeric

50g shop-bought Thai red curry paste

300g leftover cooked fish (or 500g fresh fish – see the intro)

handful of chopped fresh coriander

5–10 fresh mint leaves, chopped

While the potatoes are boiling and cooling, heat the oil in a frying pan over a medium heat. Add the ginger, garlic, fennel seeds, nigella seeds and turmeric and cook for 1 minute, then add the curry paste and stir to combine. Reduce the heat to low and cook for 3–4 minutes more, stirring constantly so that the paste doesn't stick or burn.

Flake the cooked fish into a large bowl, using this opportunity to make sure there are no bones. Add the spiced curry paste, grated potato and fresh herbs and mix until well combined. Divide into eight portions and form each one into a cake roughly 5cm across.

Heat some oil in a large non-stick frying pan over a medium heat. Working in batches if necessary so that you don't crowd the pan, add the fish cakes and cook for 5 minutes on each side, until golden brown and heated through (remember, the fish and potato are already cooked).

To serve *Serve the fish cakes with a spoonful of the masala mayo, a pinch of flaky sea salt on top and some pickled cucumbers and red onions on the side.*

SERVES 4

— TAWA JHINGA MASALA —
SPICY PRAWN CURRY

If you're craving a curry but want something lighter than usual but still full of flavour, this is the recipe for you. Tawa jhinga is meant to be a dry dish, but I've created a version that can be made at home, full of familiar ingredients but with Indian spicing.

PREP

Measure out your spices into two separate small bowls: one bowl for the whole spices and one for the ground spices and chilli flakes for the sauce.

Prep and measure out all the remaining ingredients before you start cooking so that everything is ready to go and the spices don't burn.

PREPARE THE RED ONIONS

3 red onions, peeled

Finely dice one of the red onions, then cut the other two into large bite-sized pieces. Keep the diced and chopped onions separate and set aside.

COOK THE WHOLE SPICES

60ml vegetable oil

2 fresh or dried red chillies, halved lengthways

8–10 black peppercorns

1 tsp cumin seeds

Heat the oil in a large heavy-based saucepan over a medium heat. Add the red chillies, peppercorns and cumin seeds and cook for 1 minute, stirring, until fragrant.

110   SPICE BOX

 **MAKE THE SAUCE**

1½ tsp fine sea salt

2 fresh green chillies, halved lengthways

2 tbsp grated or finely chopped garlic

1 tbsp grated or finely chopped fresh ginger

2 tbsp ground coriander

1½ tbsp paprika

1 tsp chilli flakes

½ tsp ground black pepper

¼ tsp ground turmeric

1 x 400g tin of chopped tomatoes

1 tsp caster sugar (optional)

2 peppers (red, yellow or green), cut into bite-sized pieces

16 peeled and deveined jumbo prawns

Add the finely diced red onion and the salt, reduce the heat to low and cook for a good 10 minutes, stirring occasionally, until softened and browned. Add the green chillies, garlic and ginger and cook for 1 minute.

Add the ground spices, chilli flakes and **120ml water**, stirring to combine – it will be very thick. Cook for 1 minute, then stir in the tomatoes and taste to see if you think it needs the sugar to balance out the acidity of the tomatoes. Raise the heat back up to medium and cook for 1 minute, then add the peppers, the remaining red onions and the prawns. Cook for 5–6 minutes, until the prawns are cooked through but the peppers and onions still have a lot of crunch.

 **TO FINISH**

knob of butter

1–2 spring onions, thinly sliced

chopped fresh coriander

ginger julienne

¼ tsp fine sea salt

Stir in the knob of butter, spring onions, chopped fresh coriander, ginger julienne and ¼ teaspoon of salt (or to taste). Cook for 1 minute.

To serve Serve straightaway with plain boiled basmati rice (page 204) and warm naan (shop-bought or page 211).

SERVES **4** AS A STARTER

— BHOPALI JHINGA —
CURRIED PRAWNS

This dish comes from Bhopal, a city in central India, where it's often served as a snack to have with a local drink. The smaller the prawns, the better the flavour, so I prefer to use shrimp. It's lightly spiced and as simple as can be.

PREP

Measure out your spices into two separate small bowls: one bowl for the pepper and salt and one bowl for the turmeric and paprika.

Prep and measure out all the remaining ingredients before you start cooking so that everything is ready to go and the spices don't burn.

COOK THE SHALLOTS

1 tbsp vegetable oil

1–2 large banana shallots, finely diced

1½ tsp grated or finely chopped garlic

1 tsp freshly ground black pepper

¼ tsp fine sea salt

Heat the oil in a large heavy-based frying pan over a medium heat. Add the shallots, garlic, black pepper and salt and cook for 1 minute, stirring, until the garlic is fragrant.

COOK THE PRAWNS

500g peeled and deveined black tiger prawns or shrimp

½ tsp ground turmeric

½ tsp paprika

1 lemon wedge

2 spring onions, thinly sliced

1 fresh red chilli, thinly sliced into rounds

1 tbsp chopped fresh coriander, plus extra to serve

knob of butter

Add the prawns, turmeric, paprika and **a splash of water**, then reduce the heat to medium-low and cook for a few minutes.

Squeeze in the lemon juice, then quickly cut the lemon wedge into thin slices and add them to the pan along with the spring onions and chilli. Cook for 1–2 minutes, then stir in the chopped fresh coriander. Add the knob of butter at the very end of the cooking time, tossing to coat.

To serve *Serve straightaway with thick Greek yoghurt into which you've stirred some chopped fresh coriander and a pinch of salt, then scatter some toasted flaked almonds over the prawns.*

112   SPICE BOX

SERVES **4**

— LAU CHINGRI —
PRAWN AND COURGETTE CURRY

I've used courgettes in this recipe as that is what is available to us in Ireland, but in India we use a type of squash called doodhi, which is firmer and takes longer to cook. Every Tuesday and Thursday vegetables arrive from India to be distributed to Indian shops around Ireland (there is only one vegetable distributor), so you can find it fresh in shops sometimes. This is a Bengali dish, hence the use of seafood in it too. You can't get a simpler curry than this.

PREP

Measure out your spices into two separate small bowls: one bowl for the whole spices and one for the coriander and turmeric for the curry.

Prep and measure out all the remaining ingredients before you start cooking so that everything is ready to go and the spices don't burn.

COOK THE WHOLE SPICES

40ml strong-flavoured rapeseed oil

2 fresh or dried red chillies, halved lengthways

1 tsp nigella seeds

Heat the oil in a large heavy-based saucepan over a medium heat. Add the red chillies and nigella seeds and cook for 1 minute, until fragrant. Take care not to overcook the nigella seeds here when you first temper them in the oil, otherwise they turn bitter.

MAKE THE CURRY

1 small red onion, finely diced (100g)

½ tsp fine sea salt

1 tbsp grated or finely chopped fresh ginger

1 tbsp ground coriander

½ tsp ground turmeric

1 medium courgette, quartered and very thinly sliced

1 x 400ml tin of coconut milk

400g peeled prawns

6 cherry tomatoes, halved

Add the diced onion and salt and cook for 5 minutes, stirring occasionally, until softened. Add the ginger and cook for 1 minute more.

Add the ground spices and **80ml water** so that the spices don't burn. Cook for 1 minute before stirring in the courgette and coconut milk.

Simmer for 10 minutes to bring the flavours together and reduce the coconut milk a little, then add the prawns and cook for 5 minutes.

Season with an additional pinch of salt (or to taste), then stir in the cherry tomatoes and cook for 1–2 minutes to soften a little and heat through. Remove the pan from the heat and allow the curry to settle for 5 minutes.

To serve *Serve with plain boiled basmati rice (page 204).*

SPICE BOX

SERVES **4** AS A SNACK

— MACHHI PAKORA —
PUNJABI FISH FINGERS

When I make these I always use carom seeds, but here I've called for fresh herbs that are more widely available instead. Carom seeds are used a lot in Indian cooking, but thyme is a good substitute. This is a great recipe to get kids to help with, as they like to add the crumb coating. It also makes a good alternative to frozen fish fingers.

PREP

Measure out your spices into two separate bowls: one medium bowl for the turmeric, garam masala, paprika, salt and pepper and one small bowl for the garam masala to finish.

Prep and measure out all the remaining ingredients before you start cooking so that everything is ready to go.

MAKE THE FISH FINGERS

vegetable oil, for deep-frying

1 tbsp chopped fresh dill, basil or thyme

½ tsp ground turmeric

½ tsp garam masala

¼ tsp paprika

1 tsp fine sea salt

1 tsp freshly ground black pepper

juice of 1 lime

500g cod or hake, skinned, deboned and cut into finger-size strips

75g plain flour

125g panko breadcrumbs (fresh breadcrumbs would also work)

Heat the oil in a deep-fryer to 180°C (or see the tips on page 19 if you don't have a deep-fryer).

Mix the chopped fresh herbs, ground spices, salt, pepper and lime juice in a medium bowl, then add the strips of fish and toss to coat.

Put the flour in a small bowl and whisk in **150ml water** to make a smooth paste the consistency of a thin custard. Put the breadcrumbs in a separate wide, shallow bowl.

Toss the spiced fish strips first in the batter, then transfer to the breadcrumbs and toss to coat, pressing down on the fish so that each portion is firmly and evenly coated. Set aside on a plate.

Working in batches, drop the coated fish fingers into the hot oil and deep-fry for about 5 minutes, turning over halfway through, until cooked through, crisp and golden. Using tongs, transfer to a wire rack set over a baking tray lined with kitchen paper to absorb any excess oil and stay crisp while you cook the rest.

TO FINISH

pinch of garam masala

Once all the fish fingers are cooked, sprinkle over a small pinch of garam masala and a little salt and pepper and serve hot.

SEAFOOD

SERVES **4**

— TANDOORI MACHI —
OVEN-ROASTED SEA BASS

I would always cook this in a tandoor oven, but a regular oven works too and a barbecue would be even better. Eating fish on the bone adds more flavour and keeps the fish nice and moist.

PREP

Measure out your spices into two separate small bowls: one bowl for the paprika, turmeric and salt for the first marinade and one bowl for the ground fennel, garam masala, paprika and salt for the second marinade.

Prep and measure out all the remaining ingredients before you start cooking so that everything is ready to go and the spices don't burn.

PREPARE THE FISH

1 x 450–500g whole sea bass

juice of 1 lime

Score the fish down to the bone all along its length from head to tail. Put on a large parchment-lined baking tray and drizzle over the lime juice.

MAKE THE FIRST MARINADE

1½ tsp grated or finely chopped fresh ginger

1½ tsp grated or finely chopped garlic

½ tsp paprika

½ tsp ground turmeric

1 tsp fine sea salt

Mix together the ginger, garlic, paprika, turmeric and salt, then rub this all over the fish on both sides, getting it into the slits you've cut as well. Set aside for 15–20 minutes.

MAKE THE SECOND MARINADE AND COOK

2 tbsp thick Greek yoghurt

1 tbsp rapeseed oil

½ tsp fennel seeds, ground in a pestle and mortar

½ tsp garam masala

½ tsp paprika

¼ tsp fine sea salt

In a separate bowl, whisk together all the ingredients for the second marinade – it will be very thick. Rub this all over the fish and allow to marinate for another 10 minutes.

Preheat the oven to 200°C/180°C fan/gas 6.

Roast the fish in the preheated oven for 25–30 minutes, turning the fish over halfway through. When it's done, the fish will flake apart easily when pressed.

To serve *Serve straight to the table on a serving platter with lemon rice (page 207) on the side.*

SPICE BOX

SERVES **4**

— DOI MAACH —
SALMON WITH YOGHURT, MUSTARD AND TURMERIC

When I was working in India before I moved to Ireland, we used to get Irish smoked salmon, gravlax and sometimes the whole fish and it's still one of my favourite fish. This simple recipe is a popular fish curry from Kolkata – it is mainly only in the Bengal region that you will find fish and yoghurt cooked together.

PREP

Measure out your spices into four separate small bowls: one bowl for the turmeric and salt for the yoghurt mixture; one for the whole spices; one for the coriander and turmeric for the curry; and one for the paprika, turmeric and salt for the fish.

Prep and measure out all the remaining ingredients before you start cooking so that everything is ready to go and the spices don't burn.

MAKE THE YOGHURT MIXTURE

400g thick Greek yoghurt

1 tsp ground turmeric

1 tsp fine sea salt

Whisk together the yoghurt, turmeric and salt. Pour in **600ml water** and whisk again to combine, then set aside.

COOK THE WHOLE SPICES

40ml vegetable oil

2 fresh or dried red chillies, halved lengthways

1 tsp mustard seeds

1 tsp coriander seeds

Heat the oil in a large heavy-based saucepan over a medium heat. Add the red chillies, mustard seeds and coriander seeds and cook for 1 minute, until fragrant.

MAKE THE CURRY

1 small red onion, finely diced (100g)

3 fresh green chillies, halved lengthways

1 tbsp ground coriander

1 tsp ground turmeric

juice of ½ lemon

Add the onion, chillies and a pinch of salt and cook for about 5 minutes, until softened. Add the ground coriander and turmeric and **50ml water** and cook for 1 minute, then stir in the yoghurt mixture. Bring to the boil, then reduce the heat to low and add the lemon juice. Simmer for 35–40 minutes, until thickened and reduced slightly.

ADD THE FISH

1 tbsp vegetable oil

1 tsp paprika

1 tsp ground turmeric

1 tsp fine sea salt

400g salmon, skinned and cut into thick strips

Mix the oil, paprika, turmeric and salt in a large bowl, then add the fish strips and toss to coat in the spiced oil before adding to the curry. (I like to deep-fry or pan-fry the fish before adding it to the yoghurt to help it keep its shape better, but you can add it directly to the sauce to make this a one-pot dish.) Add another **100ml water** to the curry after adding the fish to thin it a little and simmer gently for 3–4 minutes, until the fish is cooked. Remove the pan from the heat and allow the curry to settle for 5 minutes.

To serve *Garnish with a pinch of chilli flakes, then serve with plain boiled basmati rice (page 204) and baby spinach with garlic and fennel on the side (page 182).*

SERVES **4**

— MEEN CURRY —
HOME-STYLE FISH CURRY
WITH VEGETABLES

This is a mild, comforting kind of curry served without onions, garlic or ginger. You can use any root vegetable you like instead of – or in addition to – the potato and carrot. It's one of my favourite dishes.

PREP

Measure out your spices into two separate small bowls: one bowl for the whole spices and one for the cumin, paprika and turmeric for the curry.

Prep and measure out all the remaining ingredients before you start cooking so that everything is ready to go and the spices don't burn.

 **COOK THE WHOLE SPICES**

60ml vegetable oil

2–3 fresh green chillies, halved lengthways

1 tsp nigella seeds

½ tsp cumin seeds

Heat the oil in a large heavy-based saucepan over a medium heat. Add the green chillies, nigella seeds and cumin seeds and cook for 1 minute.

② MAKE THE CURRY

1 tbsp ground cumin

1 tbsp paprika

1½ tsp ground turmeric

fine sea salt

400g ripe vine
tomatoes, chopped

1 medium Maris Piper
potato, peeled and cut
into bite-sized pieces

1 carrot, cut into
bite-sized pieces

½ courgette, cut into
bite-sized pieces

½ aubergine, cut into
bite-sized pieces

500g halibut (or any
firm white fish), skin on
and cut into large
pieces

Add the ground spices, 1½ teaspoons of salt and **50ml water** to make a paste. The mixture will be thick and fragrant.

Add the tomatoes, cover the pan with a tight-fitting lid and cook for 15–20 minutes, until they've broken down. Add the potato, carrot and up to **500ml water**, depending on how much liquid the tomatoes have released – use your judgement. Cover and simmer for 10–15 minutes, until the root vegetables are soft.

Add the courgette, aubergine, fish and ½ teaspoon more salt (or to taste). Cover and simmer for 5–10 minutes, until the vegetables and fish are cooked.

③ TO FINISH

large handful of
chopped fresh
coriander

Stir in the chopped fresh coriander, remove the pan from the heat and allow the curry to settle for 5 minutes.

To serve *Serve with plain boiled basmati rice if you like (page 204), but the potatoes in it make it filling enough to eat on its own, almost like a stew.*

SEAFOOD 121

SERVES **2**

— TAWA FISH FRY —
PAN-FRIED MACKEREL

You can use any flat fish that's not too firm for this recipe because it will cook quickly and the spices won't burn. I like mackerel, but sea bass and sea bream are also good. If you were to use something thicker, like cod, the spices would be burned by the time the fish was cooked through. The semolina adds a bit of texture and creates a barrier to prevent the fish from burning, but you could use polenta instead if you need to keep the dish gluten free – or you can leave it out altogether.

PREP

Prep and measure out all the ingredients before you start cooking so that everything is ready to go and the spices don't burn.

MARINATE THE FISH

juice of ½ lime

1 tbsp rapeseed oil

1 tsp finely chopped fresh green chilli

1 tsp paprika

½ tsp ground turmeric

½ tsp ground cumin

½ tsp garam masala

½ tsp fine sea salt

4 mackerel fillets, skin on

Stir together the lime juice, rapeseed oil, green chilli, ground spices and salt into a paste. Add the mackerel fillets and toss gently to coat, then set aside to marinate for 30 minutes.

COOK THE FISH

semolina or polenta, for coating

50ml vegetable oil

1 lemon, halved

juice of ½ lime

knob of butter or ghee

Pour some semolina or polenta into a wide, shallow bowl – you don't need much as you're just dredging the fish in it. Add the fish fillets and coat evenly in the semolina on both sides, pressing to make it stick.

Heat the vegetable oil in a large, non-stick frying pan over a medium heat. Add the mackerel, skin side down, and shallow-fry for 2–3 minutes, pressing each fillet down firmly in the pan to crisp up the skin. Add the lemon halves to the hot pan too, cut side down – let them cook without moving them while you cook the fish.

Turn the fillets over, add a knob of butter or ghee to the pan and cook for 2–3 minutes more, until the fish is cooked through. Squeeze in the lime juice.

To serve *For an extra hit of sourness, garnish each plate with a charred lemon half for squeezing over at the table. Serve the fish with the pan juices spooned over and apple and fennel salad (page 199) on the side.*

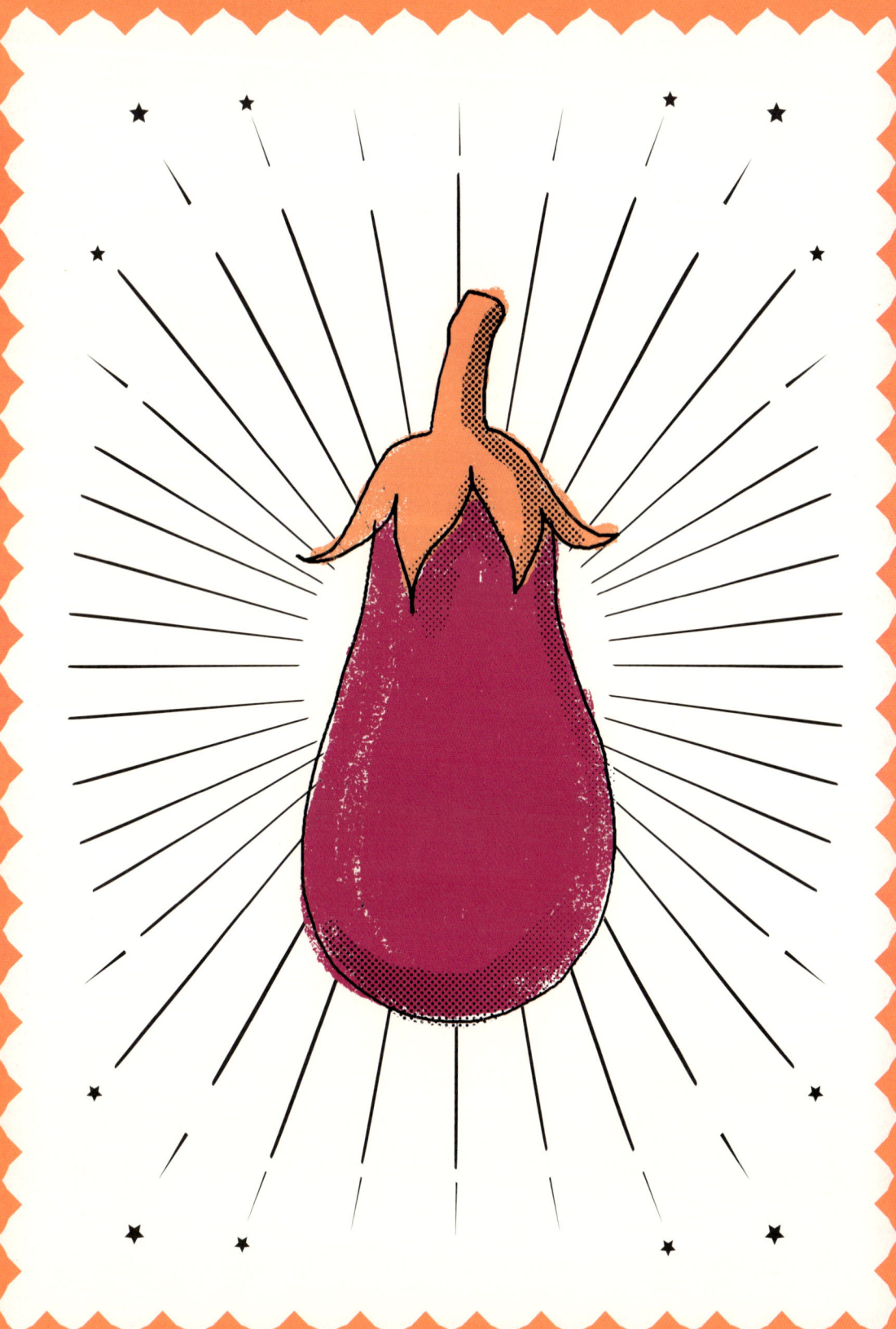

CHAPTER 4

★

VEGETARIAN MAINS

SERVES **4** TO **6**

— DAL SHORBA —
MULLIGATAWNY SOUP

This is practically the national soup of India. It was a big shock to me when I arrived in Ireland and didn't see any soups on the menus at any of the Indian restaurants; even when I put soup on my own menu, it never sold well. I think that's a shame, as there is so much goodness in a bowl of soup. Keep this vegetarian by leaving out the cooked shredded chicken at the end.

PREP

Measure out your spices into two separate small bowls: one bowl for the whole spices and one for the Madras curry powder and turmeric for the soup.

Prep and measure out all the remaining ingredients before you start cooking so that everything is ready to go and the spices don't burn.

 ## SOAK THE LENTILS

200g dried red lentils

Soak the lentils in just enough water to cover them for 20 minutes.

 ## COOK THE WHOLE SPICES

50ml vegetable oil

15–20 black peppercorns

2 star anise

1 fresh or dried red chilli, cut in half

½ tsp fennel seeds

½ tsp cumin seeds

Heat the oil in a large heavy-based saucepan over a medium heat. Add the peppercorns, star anise, red chilli, fennel seeds and cumin seeds and cook for 1 minute, until fragrant.

 ## MAKE THE SOUP

100g sliced fresh pineapple

1 small red onion, thinly sliced (70g)

1 small carrot, thinly sliced (50g)

½ green apple, cored and thinly sliced (60g)

1 fresh green chilli, halved lengthways

1 tbsp grated or finely chopped fresh ginger

1½ tsp fine sea salt

50g fresh or desiccated coconut

2 tbsp Madras curry powder

1½ tsp ground turmeric

Add the pineapple, onion, carrot, apple, green chilli, ginger and salt and cook for 5 minutes. Add the soaked lentils (including their soaking water) along with the coconut, curry powder and turmeric and **800ml water**. Bring to the boil, then reduce the heat, cover the pan and simmer for 30 minutes, stirring occasionally, until the lentils, fruit and vegetables are all completely soft.

Blend everything, including the whole spices and the red and green chillies (although you can take the chillies out at this stage if you prefer), with a hand-held blender until smooth. Stir in another **200–400ml water** to thin the soup – it shouldn't be too thick.

 ## TO FINISH

cooked basmati rice (page 204)

cooked shredded chicken (optional)

4–6 tbsp coconut milk

handful of chopped fresh coriander

1 lime, cut into wedges

Put a little rice and/or chicken (if using) in the bottom of each bowl, then pour over the soup and add an extra spoonful of rice on top. Garnish with a drizzle of coconut milk and chopped fresh coriander, then squeeze over some lime juice. Let each person stir everything together in their own bowl.

SERVES **4** TO **6**

— MALKA MASOOR DAL —
HOME-STYLE RED LENTIL DAL

When I started cooking in Ireland, I couldn't serve dal as it's served in India. Customers were always telling me that my lentils were too thin and watery, but they're made that way because the rice that dal is served with soaks up a lot of the water. I even had a customer tell me once that I should come to his house and he'd show me how to make lentils properly! Times have changed, though, and people are happy to eat them the way I make them now.

PREP

Measure out your spices into three separate small bowls: one bowl for the salt and turmeric for boiling the lentils; one bowl for the whole spices; and one bowl for the ground spices for the tadka.

Prep and measure out all the remaining ingredients before you start cooking so that everything is ready to go and the spices don't burn.

BOIL THE LENTILS

500g dried red lentils

1 garlic clove, peeled and smashed

2 tsp fine sea salt

1 tsp ground turmeric

Put the lentils in a large heavy-based saucepan with **2 litres water** and the garlic, salt and turmeric and bring to the boil. Reduce the heat and skim off any froth that rises to the top, then simmer for 20 minutes, uncovered, until the lentils are soft but haven't broken down completely. You want them to keep their shape and retain some texture – if you cook them for too long, they'll get so soft that they'll almost become a purée.

COOK THE WHOLE SPICES

50g butter or ghee

2 fresh or dried red chillies, halved lengthways

1 tsp cumin seeds

½ tsp mustard seeds

Meanwhile, melt the butter or ghee in a small saucepan over a medium heat. Add the red chillies, cumin seeds and mustard seeds and cook for 1 minute, until fragrant.

SPICE BOX

 ## MAKE THE TADKA

2 fresh green chillies, finely chopped

1 tbsp grated or finely chopped fresh ginger

1 tbsp grated or finely chopped garlic

1 tsp fine sea salt

1 tbsp ground coriander

1 tbsp paprika

½ tsp ground turmeric

1 x 400g tin of chopped tomatoes

Add the green chillies, ginger, garlic and salt and cook for 1 minute. Add the ground coriander, paprika and turmeric and stir in **50ml water** so that the spices don't burn and cook for 1 minute. Add the tomatoes and simmer, stirring once or twice, for 5 minutes. Turn the heat down to its lowest setting or remove the pan from the heat entirely so that it doesn't reduce too much.

Once the lentils are cooked, add this tomato and spice mixture (tadka) to them and bring back to the boil, again skimming off any froth that might bubble up. Cook for a few minutes to bring all the flavours together.

 ## TO FINISH

30g fresh coriander, chopped

1 lemon wedge

Stir in the chopped fresh coriander and a squeeze of lemon, then remove the pan from the heat.

To serve *Spoon one or two ladles of the dal over a bed of plain boiled basmati rice (page 204) in a serving bowl and allow to sit for 5 minutes so that the rice soaks up the liquid. Crush some shop-bought poppadums in your hands and scatter on top for extra texture.*

TIP

This makes plenty of dal, so to get another dish out of it, you can reuse some of it to make an easy red lentil soup. Remove a few ladlefuls of the lentils before you add the tadka to them. In a separate saucepan, heat 4 teaspoons of vegetable oil over a medium heat, then add ½ teaspoon cumin seeds and cook for 1 minute before adding the boiled lentils. Mash them lightly with the back of the ladle and cook for 10–15 minutes, until the lentils have completely broken down. Blend with a hand-held blender until smooth, then add a knob of butter, a little chopped fresh coriander or parsley and a squeeze of lemon juice. Serve with the garlic bread on page 218.

VEGETARIAN MAINS   129

SERVES **4**

— TADKA DAL —
RUSTIC YELLOW SPLIT PEA DAL

This is a rustic dal that my wife, Leena, makes so well. It's traditionally made with chana dal (dried split chickpeas), but yellow split peas are a good substitute that are available in supermarkets. I'm happy to eat this with basmati rice for a dinner in and of itself, but it also makes a good side dish.

PREP

Measure out your spices into three separate small bowls: one bowl for the turmeric and salt for boiling the yellow split peas; one for the coriander and fennel seeds; and one for the ground coriander, paprika and turmeric for the tadka.

Prep and measure out all the remaining ingredients before you start cooking so that everything is ready to go and the spices don't burn.

 ## COOK THE YELLOW SPLIT PEAS

200g yellow split peas (or chana dal if you can get it)

1–2 garlic cloves, peeled and smashed

1 tsp ground turmeric

1 tsp fine sea salt

Soak the yellow split peas in a large bowl of cold water for 20 minutes, then drain and rinse three times.

Put the drained split peas in a large heavy-based saucepan with **700ml fresh water** along with the garlic, turmeric and salt. Bring to the boil, then reduce the heat, cover the pan and simmer for at least 20 minutes, until the split peas are completely soft with absolutely no bite – you should be able to easily crush them between your fingers.

 ## COOK THE WHOLE SPICES

40ml vegetable oil

1 tsp coriander seeds

1 tsp fennel seeds

Meanwhile, heat the oil in a saucepan over a medium heat. Add the coriander and fennel seeds and cook for 1 minute, until fragrant.

 ## MAKE THE TADKA

1 medium red onion, finely diced

1–2 fresh green chillies, halved lengthways

1 tbsp ground coriander

1 tsp paprika

½ tsp ground turmeric

200g tomato passata or 1 x 227g tin of chopped tomatoes

2 knobs of butter

Add the onion and green chillies, increase the heat to high and cook for 2–3 minutes, stirring constantly, to brown the onions. Add the ground spices and cook for 1 minute before adding the tomatoes. Lower the heat back to medium and simmer for 5 minutes, then stir in the butter.

 ## TO FINISH

10g fresh dill, chopped (stems and all)

Once the yellow split peas are soft, stir in the tadka and the fresh dill. Remove the pan from the heat and allow the dal to settle for 5 minutes.

To serve *Serve with plain boiled basmati rice (page 204).*

VEGETARIAN MAINS

SERVES **4** TO **6**

— HYDERABADI SUBZ QURMA —
HYDERABADI VEGETABLE KORMA

I developed this recipe for all my vegan customers and friends. You can use any combination of vegetables you like, just aim for a total weight of 500 grams. To make it even easier, you could also use a frozen vegetable mix.

PREP

Measure out your spices into two separate small bowls: one bowl for the whole spices and one for the ground cardamom, fennel, turmeric and paprika for the curry.

Prep and measure out all the remaining ingredients before you start cooking so that everything is ready to go and the spices don't burn.

BLANCH THE VEGETABLES

100g carrot, sliced

100g fine green beans, sliced at an angle

100g button mushrooms, sliced

100g small cauliflower and/or broccoli florets

100g frozen petits pois

Bring a large saucepan of salted water to the boil. Add all the vegetables and boil for just 1 minute to blanch them. Drain in a colander, then put in a bowl of iced water to stop the vegetables cooking any further. Set aside.

COOK THE WHOLE SPICES

60g coconut oil

½ tsp fennel seeds

½ tsp mustard seeds

Melt the oil in a large heavy-based saucepan over a medium heat. Add the fennel and mustard seeds and cook for 1 minute, until fragrant.

132   SPICE BOX

 **MAKE THE CURRY**

1 small onion, finely diced (150g)

1 tsp fine sea salt

1 fresh green chilli, halved lengthways

4 green cardamom pods, ground in a pestle and mortar (½ tsp ground)

1 tsp fennel seeds, ground in a pestle and mortar

1 tsp ground turmeric

½ tsp paprika

50g cashew or almond butter

2 large ripe tomatoes, chopped

600ml coconut milk

Add the onion and salt and cook for about 5 minutes, until softened. Add the green chilli and cook for 1 or 2 minutes more.

Add the cardamom, fennel, turmeric and paprika and stir in **50ml water** so that the spices don't burn. Cook for 1 minute. Stir in the cashew or almond butter and tomatoes and cook for 2–3 minutes before stirring in the coconut milk.

Bring to the boil, then stir in all the drained blanched vegetables. Reduce the heat and simmer for a few minutes just to heat the vegetables through. You want them to stay crisp and vibrant, not soft and overcooked.

 **TO FINISH**

1 large ripe tomato, chopped

1 tbsp chopped fresh coriander

1 lime or lemon wedge

Add the chopped tomato and chopped fresh coriander, then squeeze in the lime or lemon juice. Remove the pan from the heat and allow the curry to settle for 5 minutes.

To serve *Serve with plain boiled basmati rice (page 204) and warm naan (shop-bought or page 211).*

SERVES **4**

— POORI BHAJI —
POTATO CURRY WITH POORI

There's a shop in the city of Agra called Shri Ram Poori Wale. When I was doing my chef training, you only got a small stipend since you were given accommodation and staff meals. But on your day off you weren't allowed to eat in the hotel, so this is the shop where I would always go. You paid for a plate of four poori but you could get unlimited vegetables, chutneys and pickles to go with it. This potato curry was one of the dishes that would be served with the poori that I could eat my fill of.

This is a popular street food breakfast in northern India, but I love to eat it at any time of day – you use the puffed balloons of poori to scoop up the curry. It's also sometimes made as part of religious meals to offer to the gods, which is why there are no onions and garlic in it.

PREP

Measure out your spices into two separate small bowls: one bowl for the whole spices and one for the ground coriander, turmeric, paprika and salt for the curry.

Prep and measure out all the remaining ingredients before you start cooking so that everything is ready to go and the spices don't burn.

COOK THE WHOLE SPICES

40ml vegetable oil

2 fresh green chillies, halved lengthways

2 cloves

1 bay leaf

1 tsp cumin seeds

Heat the oil in a large heavy-based saucepan over a medium heat. Add the green chillies, cloves, bay leaf and cumin seeds and cook for 1 minute, until fragrant.

134   SPICE BOX

 **MAKE THE CURRY**

1 tbsp ground
coriander

1 tsp ground turmeric

1 tsp paprika

1 tsp fine sea salt

500g peeled, boiled
and diced potatoes

200g ripe tomatoes,
chopped

Add the ground spices, salt and **1 tablespoon water** so that the spices don't burn. Stir together into a paste and cook for 1 minute, then add the potatoes and tomatoes, crushing them lightly with the back of the spoon. Cook for a few minutes, then add another **400ml water**. Bring to the boil, then reduce the heat and simmer gently while you cook the poori on page 205.

TO FINISH

1 lemon wedge

1 tbsp chopped fresh
coriander

Add a squeeze of lemon juice and the chopped fresh coriander to the curry. Remove the pan from the heat and allow the curry to settle for 5 minutes.

To serve *Serve with the poori (page 205) – break off portions for scooping up the curry – and shop-bought mango chutney.*

VEGETARIAN MAINS 135

SERVES **4**

— CHANA BHATURA —
CHICKPEA CURRY WITH POORI

This chickpea curry is so simple but so versatile. It's particularly good served with pickled red onions and poori (deep-fried puffed breads) for scooping up the curry, but you can't go wrong with a simple bed of plain boiled basmati rice or naan.

PREP

Measure out your spices into two separate small bowls: one bowl for the whole spices and one for the ground fennel, coriander, paprika, cumin, garam masala and ground black pepper for the curry.

Prep and measure out all the remaining ingredients before you start cooking so that everything is ready to go and the spices don't burn.

COOK THE WHOLE SPICES

70g butter, ghee or vegetable oil

8–10 black peppercorns

3–4 cloves

2 green cardamom pods

2 bay leaves

2 fresh or dried red chillies, halved lengthways

1 cinnamon stick

Melt the butter or ghee or heat the oil in a large heavy-based saucepan over a medium heat. Add the peppercorns, cloves, cardamom, bay leaves, red chillies and cinnamon stick and cook for 1 minute, until fragrant.

MAKE THE CURRY

1 large onion, finely diced (200g)

1 tsp fine sea salt

2–3 fresh green chillies, halved lengthways

1 tbsp grated or finely chopped fresh ginger

1 tbsp grated or finely chopped garlic

1 tsp fennel seeds, ground in a pestle and mortar

2 tbsp ground coriander

1 tbsp paprika

1 tsp ground cumin

1 tsp garam masala

¼ tsp freshly ground black pepper

200g tomato passata or 1 x 227g tin of chopped tomatoes

2 x 400g tins of chickpeas, drained and rinsed

Add the onion and salt and cook for about 5 minutes, until the onion is softened and lightly browned. Add the green chillies, ginger and garlic and cook for 1 minute more.

Add the ground spices and **50ml water** so that the spices don't burn. Cook for 1 minute before adding the tomatoes. Reduce the heat and simmer gently for about 10 minutes to bring all the flavours together – it will be very thick at this point.

Add the chickpeas and crush one-quarter of them with the back of the spoon, then stir in another **300ml water**. Simmer for another 5 minutes, then taste and adjust the seasoning with more salt and pepper if needed.

TO FINISH

1 fresh green chilli, finely diced

thumb-sized piece of fresh ginger, cut into matchsticks

½ small ripe tomato, chopped

juice of ½ lemon

1 tbsp chopped fresh coriander, plus extra to garnish

pinch of garam masala

Toss together the green chilli, ginger, tomato, lemon juice, fresh coriander and garam masala in a bowl. Remove the pan from the heat, stir in all the finishing ingredients and allow the curry to settle for 5 minutes.

To serve *Garnish with a little more chopped fresh coriander. Serve with pickled red onions (page 200) to add some bite, lime wedges for squeezing over and poori (page 205) for scooping up the curry.*

VEGETARIAN MAINS

SERVES **4**

— ALOO BAINGAN KA SALAN —
BENGALI BABU'S AUBERGINE AND POTATO CURRY

Babu means gentleman and in India we use the term like you would use the word 'sir'. We have a chef in the kitchen who is Bengali and my nickname for him is Bengali Babu. He loves aubergines, so I've named this dish for him. This is one of the bestselling vegetarian dishes at Street.

PREP

Measure out your spices into three separate small bowls: one bowl for the whole spices; one for the ground coriander, paprika, cumin and turmeric for the curry; and one for the ground fennel to finish.

Prep and measure out all the remaining ingredients before you start cooking so that everything is ready to go and the spices don't burn.

 ## COOK THE WHOLE SPICES

50ml rapeseed oil

2 fresh or dried red chillies, halved lengthways

2 tsp nigella seeds, plus extra to garnish

2 tsp fennel seeds

1 tsp cumin seeds

1 tsp mustard seeds

Heat the oil in a large heavy-based saucepan over a medium heat. Add the red chillies and nigella, fennel, cumin and mustard seeds and cook for 1 minute, until fragrant.

MAKE THE CURRY

1 red onion, finely diced (180g)

1½ tsp fine sea salt

1½ tbsp grated or finely chopped fresh ginger

1½ tbsp grated or finely chopped garlic

1½ tbsp ground coriander

1 tbsp paprika

1½ tsp ground cumin

1 tsp ground turmeric

50g tomato purée

1 x 400ml tin of coconut milk

1 large potato, peeled and cut into small dice

2 aubergines, cut into small dice

Add the onion and salt and cook for about 10 minutes, until softened but not browned. Add the ginger and garlic and cook for 1 minute more.

Add the ground coriander, paprika, cumin and turmeric and **100ml water** so that the spices don't burn. Cook for a few minutes, until the oil starts to separate out around the edges. Add the tomato purée and another **200ml water** and cook for 2 minutes, stirring.

Stir in the coconut milk, then add the potato. Cover the pan with a lid and cook for 10 minutes, then add the aubergines and cook for 15–20 minutes more, still covered, until the vegetables are tender. Stir every so often so that the curry doesn't catch at the bottom of the pan.

TO FINISH

6 cherry tomatoes, halved

1 tbsp chopped fresh coriander, plus extra to garnish

½ tsp fennel seeds, ground in a pestle and mortar

1 lemon wedge

Stir in the cherry tomatoes, chopped fresh coriander and ground fennel and squeeze in the lemon juice. Remove the pan from the heat and allow the curry to settle for 5 minutes.

To serve *Garnish with a little more chopped fresh coriander and a pinch of nigella seeds, then serve with plain boiled basmati rice (page 204) and warm naan (shop-bought or page 211).*

VEGETARIAN MAINS

SERVES **4**

— RAJMAH CHAWAL —
LEENA'S KIDNEY BEAN CURRY

Rajmah chawal is a classic comfort food that Punjabis in particular love just about more than anything. It's the heart and soul of any Punjabi. The best kidney beans are grown in Kashmir. My mother always made this curry with rose-coloured kidney beans, which is what were available to us, but when I got married my mother-in-law from Himachal made it with small, dark-coloured kidney beans and the flavour was completely different – and, I must admit, better.

PREP

Measure out your spices into two separate small bowls: one bowl for the whole spices and one for the ground coriander, fennel, ginger and paprika for the curry.

Prep and measure out all the remaining ingredients before you start cooking so that everything is ready to go and the spices don't burn.

 ## COOK THE WHOLE SPICES

80ml rapeseed oil

2 fresh or dried red chillies, halved lengthways

1–2 cloves

1 tsp fennel seeds

Heat the oil in a large heavy-based saucepan over a medium heat. Add the red chillies, cloves and fennel seeds and cook for 1 minute, until fragrant.

 ## MAKE THE CURRY

1 large onion, finely diced

1 tsp fine sea salt

1 tbsp grated or finely chopped fresh ginger

1 tbsp grated or finely chopped garlic

1½ tbsp ground coriander

1½ tsp ground fennel

1½ tsp ground ginger

1 tsp paprika

100g natural yoghurt

200g tomato passata or 1 x 227g tin of chopped tomatoes

2 x 400g tins of red kidney beans, drained and rinsed

1 tbsp finely chopped fresh green chilli

Add the onion and salt and cook for 5–8 minutes, until softened and translucent. Add the ginger and garlic and cook for 1 minute more.

Add the ground spices and **50ml water** so that the spices don't burn. Cook for 1 minute, then stir in the yoghurt and cook for 1 minute more. Add the tomatoes and simmer for 5 minutes, then add the kidney beans and green chilli, mashing the beans a little with the back of the spoon before stirring in another **400ml water**. Bring to the boil, then lower the heat and simmer for 10 minutes, until slightly reduced.

TO FINISH

1 tbsp chopped fresh coriander, plus extra to garnish

knob of butter

1 lemon wedge

Remove the saucepan from the heat, then add the fresh coriander and the butter to give the curry a nice shine. Allow to settle for 5 minutes before squeezing in the lemon juice for a final bit of brightness.

To serve *Garnish with a little chopped fresh coriander and ½ small red onion, thinly sliced. Serve with plain boiled basmati rice (page 204).*

SERVES **4**

— AKURI —
INDIAN SCRAMBLED EGGS

We often make this for breakfast when we arrive to work in the morning at the restaurants, scooped up with roti hot off the pan.

PREP

Prep and measure out all your spices and ingredients into separate bowls before you start cooking so that everything is ready to go and the spices don't burn: one bowl for the red onion, green chilli, ginger, cumin seeds and salt; one bowl for the chopped tomato; one bowl for the ground coriander, paprika and turmeric; a bowl or jug for the beaten eggs; and one small bowl for the chopped fresh coriander.

MAKE THE SCRAMBLED EGGS

30g butter or ghee

2 tbsp vegetable oil

1 large red onion, finely diced

1 fresh green chilli, finely diced

1 tbsp grated or finely chopped fresh ginger

½ tsp cumin seeds

½ tsp fine sea salt

1 large ripe tomato, chopped

1 tsp ground coriander

1 tsp paprika

½ tsp ground turmeric

8 large eggs, beaten

Melt the butter or ghee with the oil in a large non-stick frying pan over a medium heat. Add the red onion, green chilli, ginger, cumin seeds and salt and cook for 5 minutes, until the onion has softened. Add the tomato and cook for a few minutes more.

Add the ground spices and cook for 1 minute, stirring, then pour in the beaten eggs and immediately reduce the heat to low. Cook until the eggs are softly scrambled and cooked through, stirring constantly so that big lumps don't have a chance to form – you want the eggs to be nice and creamy.

TO FINISH

handful of chopped fresh coriander

Fold in the chopped fresh coriander.

To serve *Serve hot with freshly made roti (page 214) and your favourite shop-bought lime pickle.*

142   SPICE BOX

SERVES **4**

— ANDA CURRY —
EGG CURRY

Many years ago the food writer Alex Meehan asked me if I'd serve egg curry, as he had fond memories of his father making it. I thought it was such a simple dish that no one would want to order it, but I put it on my menu just for him.

> ### PREP
>
> Measure out your spices into four separate small bowls: one bowl for the turmeric and paprika for the eggs; one for the whole spices; one for the ground coriander, paprika, cumin, turmeric and mace or nutmeg for the curry; and one for the garam masala to finish.
>
> Prep and measure out all the remaining ingredients before you start cooking so that everything is ready to go and the spices don't burn.

COOK THE EGGS

4–8 eggs

pinch of ground turmeric

pinch of paprika

1 tbsp vegetable oil

To hard-boil the eggs, place them in a medium saucepan and add enough cold water to cover them by about 1cm. Bring the water to the boil, then reduce the heat to a simmer and cook for 6 minutes for a softer yolk and 7 minutes if you like it to be cooked through. As soon as they are cooked, drain and cool them rapidly under cold running water before peeling and leaving whole.

Lightly score each peeled hard-boiled egg three or four times on one side with a small sharp knife, then place in a bowl with a pinch of turmeric and paprika and toss to coat. Heat the tablespoon of oil in a frying pan over a medium heat. Add the eggs and cook for 2 minutes just to give them a bit of colour and to crisp up the outside a bit. Set aside.

COOK THE WHOLE SPICES

50ml vegetable oil

3–4 green cardamom pods

2 cloves

2 bay leaves

1 fresh or dried red chilli, halved lengthways

½ tsp cumin seeds

Heat the oil in a large heavy-based saucepan over a medium heat. Add the cardamom pods, cloves, bay leaves, red chilli and cumin seeds and cook for 1 minute, until fragrant.

SPICE BOX

 ## MAKE THE CURRY

2 large red onions,
finely diced (300g)

2 tsp fine sea salt

1 fresh green chilli,
halved lengthways

1 tbsp grated or finely
chopped fresh ginger

1 tbsp grated or finely
chopped garlic

1½ tbsp ground
coriander

1½ tsp paprika

1 tsp ground cumin

1 tsp ground turmeric

pinch of ground mace
or nutmeg

2 large ripe tomatoes,
chopped (200g)

1 tbsp tomato purée

Add the onions and salt and cook for 5–8 minutes, until softened. Add the green chilli, ginger and garlic and cook for 2 minutes more.

Add the ground spices and **50ml water** so that the spices don't burn. Cook for 1 minute, then add the tomatoes and cook for a few minutes more, until they've started to soften. Stir in the tomato purée and cook for 1–2 minutes to cook out its raw flavour, then pour in another **400ml water** and stir to combine.

Simmer for 15–20 minutes, until the sauce has reduced and thickened a little, then blend briefly, including the whole spices and halved chillies, with a hand-held blender. You don't want it to be completely smooth; there should still be plenty of texture. This curry is also quite thin because it's traditionally served with lots of rice.

  ## TO FINISH

40ml cream

1 lemon wedge

handful of chopped
fresh coriander

pinch of garam
masala

Stir the cream into the curry, then add the eggs and simmer for a few minutes, until they've heated through. Add a squeeze of lemon, then fold in the chopped fresh coriander and a pinch of garam masala. Remove the pan from the heat and allow the curry to settle for 5 minutes.

To serve *Serve with plain boiled basmati rice (page 204) and warm naan (shop-bought or page 211).*

VEGETARIAN MAINS   145

SERVES **4**

— PALAK PANEER —
SAAG PANEER

This dish is always called saag paneer on Indian menus here, but it's called palak paneer in India (saag actually means mustard leaves, while palak is spinach). My father loved the version with mustard leaves so much that when they came into season, he'd come home from the market with 10 kilograms of the leaves to make this curry. He could eat it morning, noon and night. It's one of the most popular vegetarian dishes in India – you'll find it everywhere, from street food to fine dining. This is my mother's recipe.

PREP

Measure out your spices into three separate small bowls: one bowl for the whole spices; one for the ground fennel, paprika and salt for the curry; and one for the mace or nutmeg to finish.

Prep and measure out all the remaining ingredients before you start cooking so that everything is ready to go and the spices don't burn.

MAKE THE CORIANDER AND CHILLI PURÉE

3–4 fresh green chillies, halved lengthways

40g fresh coriander (including the stems)

4 large garlic cloves, roughly chopped

50ml vegetable oil

Put the green chillies, fresh coriander (stems and all), garlic and oil in a food processor or blender and blitz until smooth. You might need to add **1–2 tablespoons of water** to get it to blend. Scrape out into a bowl.

MAKE THE SPINACH PURÉE

500g frozen spinach, thawed

Blend the thawed spinach with any water that has come out of it (in other words, don't squeeze out the water) in the food processor or blender until smooth, again adding **1–2 tablespoons of water** if necessary to get it to blend. Scrape out into a separate bowl.

 ## COOK THE WHOLE SPICES

1 tbsp butter or ghee

2 fresh or dried red chillies, halved lengthways

1 tsp cumin seeds

Melt the butter or ghee in a large saucepan over a medium heat. Add the red chillies and cumin seeds and cook for 1 minute, until fragrant, then reduce the heat to very low, add the coriander and chilli purée and cook for a few minutes more.

 ## MAKE THE CURRY

1 tbsp ground fennel

1½ tsp paprika

1 tsp fine sea salt

150g ripe tomatoes, chopped

2 x 200g packs of paneer cheese, diced

100ml cream

Add the ground spices and salt and cook for 1 minute, then stir in the tomatoes and the spinach purée, crushing the tomatoes a bit with the back of the spoon. Increase the heat back to medium and cook for 10 minutes, stirring occasionally, to cook out the raw taste of the spinach. The curry will be very thick at this point. Add the paneer and **80ml water** and simmer for 1–2 minutes before stirring in the cream. It will still be quite thick, but this curry is meant to be thick because it's traditionally served with only naan, roti or aloo paratha, not rice.

TO FINISH

2 knobs of butter

pinch of ground mace or nutmeg

Stir in the butter and a pinch of ground mace or nutmeg. Remove the pan from the heat and allow the curry to settle for 5 minutes.

To serve *Serve with warm naan (shop-bought or page 211), roti (page 214) or aloo paratha (page 216).*

VEGETARIAN MAINS   149

MAKES **2** TO **3** WRAPS

— KOLKATA KATHI KEBAB —
VEGETABLE ROLL

In India this is served as street food that gets wrapped up in parchment so that you can eat it on the go. You can add anything you want to this, such as tofu, baby spinach, broccoli or fine green beans. And if the wraps and spread you use are vegan, then these rolls are vegan too. Or to go in the opposite direction, if you have any leftover tandoori-style chicken (page 42) or chicken jalfrezi (page 46), use that in the roll.

PREP

Measure out your spices into three separate small bowls: one bowl for the whole spices; one for the ground coriander, paprika and cumin for the stir-fried vegetables; and one for the garam masala to finish.

Prep and measure out all the remaining ingredients before you start cooking so that everything is ready to go and the spices don't burn.

COOK THE WHOLE SPICES

40ml vegetable oil

1–2 bay leaves

½ tsp cumin seeds

Heat the oil in a large frying pan over a medium heat. Add the bay leaves and cumin seeds and cook for 1 minute, until fragrant.

150   SPICE BOX

 **STIR-FRY THE VEGETABLES**

1 small red onion, thinly sliced

1 tsp fine sea salt

1 fresh green chilli, finely chopped

1 tbsp grated or finely chopped fresh ginger

1½ tsp grated or finely chopped garlic

1½ tsp ground coriander

1½ tsp paprika

1 tsp ground cumin

1 tbsp tomato purée

1 red, yellow or green pepper, thinly sliced

1 large carrot, julienned

½ courgette, julienned

1 tbsp chopped fresh coriander

pinch of garam masala

Add the onion and salt and cook for about 5 minutes, until the onion has softened. Add the green chilli, ginger and garlic and cook for 1 minute more.

Add the ground spices and **1 tablespoon of water** so that the spices don't burn. Cook for 1 minute before adding the tomato purée and cooking for 2 minutes more to cook out the raw flavour.

Add the peppers, carrot and courgette, increase the heat to high and stir-fry for no more than 5 minutes. I hate to see vegetables dying by overcooking them, so take the pan off the heat after 5 minutes and leave it for a few minutes and the vegetables will be perfectly cooked – softened but still with a little bite. Remove and discard the bay leaves, then stir in the chopped fresh coriander and a pinch of garam masala.

 **ASSEMBLE THE ROLLS**

2–3 large white wraps

mint and coriander chutney (page 224), ketchup or mayonnaise

2 tbsp vegetable oil

Put a wrap on the countertop and spread a little mint chutney, ketchup or mayonnaise all over it, right to the edges. Spoon a line of vegetables along the short side of the wrap that's closest to you and roll it up once or twice, then fold in both ends to enclose the filling and keep rolling all the way to the end. Repeat with the remaining wraps and filling.

Heat the 2 tablespoons of vegetable oil in a large non-stick frying pan over a medium-high heat. Add the wraps to the pan, seam side down, and cook for a few minutes on each side, until golden and a little crisp.

Cut each wrap on the diagonal and serve warm.

SERVES **4**

— MATAR PANEER —
PANEER AND PEA CURRY

This classic pea and paneer curry is a special occasion dish for vegetarian families.
You can easily make it vegan by using tofu instead of paneer and using coconut
milk instead of the cream and yoghurt.

PREP

Measure out your spices into three separate small bowls: one bowl for the whole
spices; one for the ground coriander, paprika, cumin and turmeric for the curry; and
one for the garam masala to finish.

Prep and measure out all the remaining ingredients before you start cooking so
that everything is ready to go and the spices don't burn.

 ## COOK THE WHOLE SPICES

80ml vegetable oil

3–4 green cardamom pods

1–2 bay leaves

2 cloves

1 small cinnamon stick, broken up

1 tsp cumin seeds

Heat the oil in a large heavy-based saucepan over a medium heat. Add the green cardamom, bay leaves, cloves, cinnamon stick and cumin seeds and cook for 1 minute, until fragrant.

MAKE THE CURRY

1 large onion, finely diced

1 tsp fine sea salt

2 fresh green chillies, finely chopped

1 tbsp grated or finely chopped fresh ginger

1 tbsp grated or finely chopped garlic

3 tbsp ground coriander

1 tbsp paprika

1 tsp ground cumin

1 tsp ground turmeric

1 x 400g tin of chopped tomatoes

50g thick Greek yoghurt

400g paneer cheese, diced into bite-sized cubes

300g frozen petits pois

Add the onion and salt and cook for 5–8 minutes, until the onion is softened and nicely browned. Add the green chillies, ginger and garlic and cook for 1 minute more.

Add the ground spices and **50ml water** so that the spices don't burn. Cook for 2 minutes over a gentle heat, then stir in the tomatoes and yoghurt. Simmer for 5 minutes, then thin the sauce with another **200ml water**. Blitz everything with a hand-held blender, including the whole spices and bay leaves, until smooth.

Add the paneer and peas. Bring up to the boil, then reduce the heat and simmer for 5–10 minutes, until the paneer has softened.

TO FINISH

50ml cream (optional)

1 tbsp chopped fresh coriander

¼ tsp garam masala

Stir in the cream (if using), chopped fresh coriander and garam masala. Remove the pan from the heat and allow the curry to settle for 5 minutes.

To serve *Serve with plain boiled basmati rice (page 204) and warm naan (shop-bought or page 211).*

MAKES **6** TO **8** SKEWERS

— PANEER TIKKA —
PANEER CHEESE SKEWERS

It goes without saying that these would be even better cooked on a barbecue on a hot summer day. Traditionally the skewers are served with only paneer, peppers and onions, but you could add fruit to the skewers as well, like pineapple or apple, or other vegetables, like aubergines or boiled baby potatoes.

PREP

Measure out your spices into three separate small bowls: one bowl for all the seeds in the first marinade; one for the paprika, turmeric, chilli flakes and salt for the first marinade; and one for the turmeric, paprika, fennel and salt for the second marinade.

Prep and measure out all the remaining ingredients before you start cooking so that everything is ready to go and the spices don't burn.

1 PREPARE THE CHEESE AND VEGETABLES

3 x 200g packs of paneer cheese, cut into thick slices

4 red, yellow and/or orange peppers

2 large red onions

Cut a pocket into each thick slice of paneer cheese by slicing it in half but without cutting all the way through. Cut the peppers into large pieces. Peel the onions and cut into thick wedges.

154   SPICE BOX

 ## MAKE THE FIRST MARINADE

1 tbsp coriander seeds

1½ tsp fennel seeds

1 tsp cumin seeds

1 tsp nigella seeds

½ tsp mustard seeds

50ml rapeseed oil

1 tbsp paprika

1 tsp ground turmeric

½ tsp chilli flakes

1 tsp fine sea salt

1½ tsp grated or finely chopped fresh ginger

1½ tsp grated or finely chopped garlic

2 tbsp malt vinegar

To make the first marinade, put all the seeds on a chopping board, then roll over them a few times with a rolling pin to lightly crush them (or use a pestle and mortar). Transfer to a large bowl, then add the oil, paprika, turmeric, chilli flakes, salt, ginger, garlic and vinegar and mix into a paste.

Add the paneer, tossing to coat and making sure you get the marinade into the pocket that you cut into the paneer, then add the peppers and onions and toss to coat them too. Cover the bowl with cling film and marinate in the fridge for at least 30 minutes, but preferably 1–2 hours or overnight.

 ## ASSEMBLE AND COOK

100g thick Greek yoghurt

50ml cream

1 tsp vegetable oil, plus extra for brushing

½ tsp ground turmeric

½ tsp paprika

½ tsp fennel seeds, ground in a pestle and mortar

¼ tsp fine sea salt

Mix the yoghurt, cream, oil, ground spices and salt together, then drizzle it over the paneer, peppers and onions and toss to coat.

Preheat the oven to 240°C/220°C fan/gas 9. Line two baking trays with foil.

To assemble, thread an onion wedge (or a few separate petals, as inevitably some of the wedges will break apart) on to a metal or wooden skewer, followed by a slice of paneer and a pepper. Repeat with another onion, slice of paneer and pepper, then add one last onion to finish the skewer.

Divide the skewers between the two lined baking trays. Cook in the oven for 12–15 minutes, until the vegetables are starting to char. Turn over the skewers as best you can (some of the vegetables and paneer won't want to flip), return to the oven and cook for 10 minutes more, until nicely charred.

Alternatively, you could brush the ridges of a griddle pan with vegetable oil and set it over a high heat. When the pan is good and hot, add one or two skewers (depending on the size of your pan – you don't want to overcrowd it) and cook for 3–4 minutes on each side without touching them, until the vegetables and paneer are nicely charred with defined grill marks but the onions and peppers still have some crunch.

To serve *Serve while the skewers are still hot with warm naan (shop-bought or page 211) and mint and coriander chutney (page 224) on the side.*

MAKES **8** TO **10**

— ALOO TIKKI —
STUFFED POTATO CAKES

When we were kids, if it was someone's birthday my mother would take us to shop in nearby Maharaj Bada rather than our local shops – it would be a treat, like shopping on Grafton Street in Dublin. There is one shop there, S.S. Kachori Wala, that specialises in making potato cakes and samosas. It's so popular that it can create traffic jams because of the number of people who want to get their food there. My father took me there for the first time in the early 1990s and insisted that I try their potato cakes – I'd never eaten anything like it and I still go to that same shop every time I'm back in India.

Every street food vendor in India serves potato cakes with something delicious to go with them and they've been on the menu of every restaurant I've ever worked in – they've never let me down. I like to have them with the chickpea curry on page 136, but they're also good on their own with this sweet-and-sour yoghurt and mint and coriander chutney.

PREP

Measure out your spices into two separate small bowls: one bowl for the cumin seeds for the stuffing and one for the ground coriander, garam masala, salt and pepper.

Prep and measure out all the remaining ingredients before you start cooking so that everything is ready to go and the spices don't burn.

COOK THE POTATOES

4 Maris Piper potatoes (750g), peeled

Boil the whole peeled potatoes for 15–20 minutes, until completely cooked through. Allow to cool, then grate with the large holes on a box grater and set aside.

MAKE THE SWEET-AND-SOUR YOGHURT

200g natural yoghurt

juice of ½ lime

1 tbsp caster sugar

1 tsp fine sea salt

Meanwhile, stir together the yoghurt, lime juice, sugar and salt in a small bowl. Cover the bowl with cling film and set aside in the fridge until ready to serve.

SPICE BOX

 ## MAKE THE STUFFING

100g frozen petits pois

knob of butter

¼ tsp cumin seeds

1 fresh green chilli, finely chopped

1 tsp grated or finely chopped fresh ginger

1½ tsp chopped fresh coriander

½ tsp ground coriander

pinch of garam masala

¼ tsp fine sea salt

pinch of freshly ground black pepper

To make the stuffing, boil the frozen peas for just 1 minute, then drain and lightly crush with a potato masher.

Melt the butter in a large frying pan over a medium heat. Add the cumin seeds, green chilli and ginger and cook for 1 minute, until fragrant. Add the crushed peas, then stir in the chopped fresh coriander, ground spices and the salt and pepper. Tip out on to a plate to cool slightly.

 ## MAKE THE POTATO CAKES

1 fresh green chilli, finely chopped

50g fresh breadcrumbs

1 tbsp melted butter

2 tsp grated or finely chopped fresh ginger

½ tsp fine sea salt

To make the potato cakes, use your hands to thoroughly mix the grated potato, green chilli, breadcrumbs, melted butter, ginger and salt until smooth and firm, almost like a dough. Take a 60g portion, form it into a ball and then make a deep indent in the middle of it with your thumb. Fill with 1 teaspoon of the stuffing, then form the potato around the peas to completely enclose the filling. Flatten into a disc, then roll the edges of the disc along your countertop like it's a wheel to get the perfect shape. Repeat with the remaining potato and stuffing mixture.

 ## COOK THE POTATO CAKES

vegetable oil, for deep-frying or pan-frying

If you're deep-frying the potato cakes, which is how we serve them in my restaurants, heat the oil in your deep-fryer to 180°C (or see the tips on page 19 if you don't have a deep-fryer). Working in batches, fry them in the hot oil for 3–4 minutes, until crisp and an even golden brown all over.

If you're pan-frying the cakes, heat 1 tablespoon of oil in a large non-stick frying pan over a medium heat. Working in batches so that you don't crowd the pan, add the potato cakes and fry for about 4 minutes on each side without disturbing them, until crisp and golden brown. Add more oil if required for the next batch.

To serve *Serve the potato cakes while still warm with the sweet and sour yoghurt and a drizzle of mint and coriander chutney (page 224), then top with a few red onion slices and garnish with a handful of chopped fresh coriander.*

VEGETARIAN MAINS   159

SERVES **2**

— GOBHI MUSALLAM —
SPICED WHOLE ROASTED CAULIFLOWER

When I was young, I had a friend whose family owned a farm and we used to buy produce directly from them. If I went back to his farm with him after school, I'd pick mooli (a type of large white radish) straight from the ground, wash it and eat it raw. We bought our cauliflower from his farm, which I would bring back home on my bicycle.

Cauliflower is a highly underrated vegetable and I never saw it being served in any Indian restaurants in Ireland 20 years ago, only yellow lentils, chickpeas, potatoes and sometimes cabbage. But it needs to be cooked properly, with some crunch still left – if you overcook it and it becomes too soft, it loses all its flavour. You can serve this as a main course or it makes a fantastic kebab.

PREP

Measure out your spices into three separate small bowls: one bowl for the cloves, star anise, turmeric and salt for boiling the cauliflower; one for the turmeric, paprika, cloves and salt for the yoghurt coating; and one for the garam masala to finish.

Prep and measure out all the remaining ingredients before you start cooking so that everything is ready to go and the spices don't burn.

BOIL THE CAULIFLOWER

2 heads of baby
cauliflower or
1 large head

4 cloves

2 star anise

1 tsp ground turmeric

½ tsp fine sea salt

Preheat the oven to 220°C/200°C fan/gas 7. Line a baking tray with foil.

Put the cauliflower in a medium saucepan with **1 litre water** and the cloves, star anise, turmeric and salt. Cover the pan with a lid and bring to the boil. Reduce the heat and simmer for 5–10 minutes, until the tip of a sharp knife can pierce through the centre of the cauliflower without too much resistance, but don't let it get too soft or it won't hold its shape well when you roast it. Drain well.

MAKE THE YOGHURT COATING

80g thick Greek
yoghurt

1 fresh green chilli,
finely chopped

½ tsp ground turmeric

¼ tsp paprika

pinch of ground cloves

½ tsp fine sea salt

Mix all the ingredients for the yoghurt coating together in a large bowl. Add the drained cauliflower and cover it all over in a thick layer of the yoghurt.

ROAST THE CAULIFLOWER

melted butter

Place the cauliflower on the lined baking tray and roast in the preheated oven for 20 minutes, then remove and baste all over with melted butter. Return to the oven and roast for about 10 minutes more, until nicely charred.

TO FINISH

1 lemon wedge

pinch of garam
masala

Transfer the cauliflower to a serving plate and finish with a squeeze of lemon juice and a pinch of garam masala on top.

To serve *Drizzle with one or two spoonfuls of mint and coriander chutney (page 224) and serve extra on the side.*

VEGETARIAN MAINS   163

CHAPTER 5

SALADS,
SIDES AND
SNACKS

SERVES **4**

— SUNDAL —
WARM CHICKPEA, MANGO AND COCONUT SALAD

For the millennium New Year back in 1999, when I was still working in India, we created a special menu at the hotel I was working at to celebrate the old but also welcome the new. The chef asked me to create seven salads from each of the four corners of India (north, east, south, west) to make 28 salads in total. I didn't know any salad recipes, so I asked all the staff in the hotel – reception, other chefs, housekeeping – for suggestions. I got this recipe from one of the women working front of house.

PREP

Prep and measure out all the spices and ingredients before you start cooking so that everything is ready to go and the spices don't burn.

1 COOK THE WHOLE SPICES

2 tbsp vegetable oil

2 fresh or dried red chillies, halved lengthways

1 tsp mustard seeds

Heat the oil in a large frying pan over a medium heat. Add the red chillies and mustard seeds and cook for 1 minute, until fragrant.

2 MAKE THE SALAD

50g fresh coconut shavings or dried coconut flakes

1 small shallot, very finely diced

½ tsp fine sea salt

1 x 400g tin of chickpeas, drained and rinsed

pinch of ground turmeric

1 ripe mango, peeled and diced

8 cherry tomatoes, halved

1 tbsp finely chopped fresh coriander

1 lime, cut into wedges

pinch of garam masala

Add the coconut, shallot and salt and cook for 1 minute more, then add the chickpeas and turmeric and cook for 2–3 minutes to warm the chickpeas through. Tip out into a bowl, using a spatula to scrape out every last bit from the pan.

Using a spatula, gently fold in the mango, cherry tomatoes, chopped fresh coriander, a squeeze of lime juice and a pinch of garam masala.

To serve *Serve warm with the remaining lime wedges on the side.*

166   SPICE BOX

SERVES **2** TO **4** AS A SIDE

— MUMBAI ALOO MASALA —
BOMBAY POTATOES

This may be the most famous potato dish on Indian menus
in Ireland and elsewhere. This is my version.

PREP

Measure out your spices into two separate small bowls: one bowl for the whole
spices and one for the ground coriander, turmeric and paprika.

Prep and measure out all the remaining ingredients before you start cooking so
that everything is ready to go and the spices don't burn.

 ## COOK THE POTATOES

2–3 large Rooster
potatoes, peeled
(500g cooked weight)

Boil the whole potatoes for about 15 minutes, until soft and completely
cooked through. When they are cool enough to handle, cut into bite-sized
pieces. You need about 500g of cooked, diced potato.

 ## COOK THE WHOLE SPICES

2 tbsp vegetable oil

2 fresh or dried red
chillies, halved
lengthways

1½ tsp mustard seeds

Heat the oil in a large frying pan over a medium heat. Add the red chillies
and mustard seeds and cook for 1 minute, until the seeds start to pop.
Mustard seeds can burn and turn bitter very quickly, so watch them carefully.

 ## BRING IT ALL TOGETHER

80g red-skinned
peanuts or cashews

½ small red onion,
thinly sliced (80g)

1 tsp fine sea salt

2 fresh green chillies,
halved lengthways

1 tbsp grated or finely
chopped fresh ginger

1 tbsp ground
coriander

1 tsp ground turmeric

1 tsp paprika

Add the peanuts or cashews and toast for 1–2 minutes. Add the onion and
salt and cook for 5 minutes, until softened. Add the green chillies and ginger
and cook for 1 minute, until fragrant.

   Add the ground spices and **1 tablespoon of water** so that the spices don't
burn. Cook for 1 minute before adding the potato, stirring to coat in all the
spices, then add another **tablespoon of water**. Crush the potatoes a little
with the back of the spoon and continue to cook, tossing occasionally and
scraping the bottom of the pan, until the potatoes are heated through.

4 TO FINISH

1 medium ripe tomato,
chopped

large handful of
chopped fresh
coriander, plus extra
to garnish

knob of butter

Add the tomatoes, coriander and butter to the pan, tossing to coat until the
butter has melted. Cook for 1–2 minutes more, then tip out into a serving dish,
garnish with a little more chopped fresh coriander and serve straightaway.

SALADS, SIDES AND SNACKS 169

SERVES **2** TO **4** AS A SIDE

— ALOO CHAAT —
POTATOES WITH FRESH HERBS AND POMEGRANATE

This recipe is a good example of how versatile and delicious the humble potato can be. Use sweet potatoes for a different take on this classic dish. We serve it as a starter at Street.

PREP

Measure out your fresh herbs and spices into three separate small bowls: one bowl for the fresh herbs, one for the whole spices and one for the chilli flakes.

Prep and measure out all the remaining ingredients before you start cooking so that everything is ready to go and the spices don't burn.

 ## COOK THE POTATOES

2–3 large Rooster potatoes, peeled (500g cooked weight)

Boil the whole potatoes for about 15 minutes, until soft and completely cooked through. When they are cool enough to handle, cut into bite-sized pieces. You should have 500g of cooked, diced potato.

 ## PREPARE THE FRESH HERBS

15g fresh coriander

5g fresh mint

5g fresh basil

5g fresh dill

Roughly tear or chop the fresh herbs, stems and all (except for the mint), and mix together. Set aside.

 ## COOK THE WHOLE SPICES

2 tbsp vegetable oil

2–3 fresh or dried red chillies, halved lengthways

1 tbsp coriander seeds

Heat the oil in a large frying pan over a medium heat. Add the red chillies and coriander seeds and cook for 1 minute, until fragrant.

 ## BRING IT ALL TOGETHER

2 fresh green chillies, halved lengthways

½ tsp fine sea salt

70g pomegranate seeds

¼ tsp chilli flakes

1 lemon wedge

Add the green chillies and salt and cook for 1 minute more before adding the diced potato and tossing together.

Add the fresh herbs, pomegranate seeds and chilli flakes, then squeeze in the lemon juice. Stir to coat the potatoes in all the herbs and continue to cook, tossing occasionally and scraping the bottom of the pan, until the potatoes are heated through. No water is added to these potatoes, so they tend to stick.

TO FINISH

knob of butter (optional)

freshly ground black pepper

Finish with a knob of butter (if using) and some freshly ground black pepper. Tip out into a serving dish and serve straightaway, while the herbs and pomegranate seeds are still fresh and vibrant.

SERVES **4** TO **6** AS A SNACK

– SAMOSAS, THREE WAYS –

My wife, Leena, is obsessed with samosas. When she went to school, there was a small shop that sold samosas where she always called in to buy some, either on her way to school or afterwards on the way home.

Every 100km you travel in India, the samosa filling will be different even though the shape is the same. A potato filling can be found everywhere, but the spicing and additional extras, like raisins or cashews, will vary. The potato filling is the perfect way to use up leftover mashed potatoes, while the spinach and sultana filling goes in a completely different direction with a hint of sweetness and the lamb filling is more substantial. Make all three of them or just one depending on what you have to hand or how much time you have.

PREP

Prep and measure out all the spices and ingredients before you start cooking so that everything is ready to go and the spices don't burn.

FOR THE POTATO FILLING

40ml vegetable oil

1 tsp coriander seeds

½ tsp cumin seeds

½ tsp chilli flakes

1 tbsp grated or
finely chopped
fresh ginger

400g mashed
potatoes

1 tbsp ground
coriander

½ tsp fennel seeds,
ground in a pestle
and mortar

¼ tsp paprika

½ tsp fine sea salt

1–2 fresh green
chillies, finely
chopped

handful of sultanas

handful of cashews,
roughly chopped

handful of chopped
fresh coriander

1 lemon wedge

Heat the oil in a large frying pan over a medium heat. Add the coriander and cumin seeds and the chilli flakes and cook for 1 minute, until fragrant, then add the ginger and cook for 1 minute more. Add the mashed potatoes and mix to combine, then sprinkle the ground spices and salt around the edge of the pan, not on top of the mashed potatoes, to let them cook for 1 minute. Stir in the green chillies, sultanas, cashews, fresh coriander and a squeeze of lemon, then tip out into a bowl.

FOR THE SPINACH AND SULTANA FILLING

1 x 450g bag of frozen
spinach, thawed

260g feta cheese,
diced

60g sultanas

40g pine nuts

4 tsp caster sugar

1 tsp chilli flakes

Put the thawed frozen spinach in a colander set in the sink and squeeze out as much water as possible. Put the spinach, feta, sultanas, pine nuts, sugar and chilli flakes in a large bowl and use your hands to mix it all together, gently crumbling the feta as you do. Taste it – it should be slightly sweet from the sugar.

FOR THE LAMB FILLING

2 tbsp vegetable oil

½ tsp coriander
seeds

½ tsp cumin seeds

½ tsp fennel seeds

2 tbsp very finely
diced red onion

1 tbsp finely
chopped fresh
green chilli

1 tbsp grated or
finely chopped
fresh ginger

1 tsp fine sea salt

1 tbsp ground
coriander

1½ tsp paprika

pinch of ground
turmeric

200g lamb mince

30g cashews,
roughly chopped

3–4 fresh mint
leaves, shredded

Heat the oil in a large frying pan over a medium heat. Add the coriander, cumin and fennel seeds and cook for 1 minute, until fragrant. Add the red onion, green chilli, ginger and salt and cook for about 5 minutes, until the onion has softened. Add the ground spices and cook for 1 minute, then add the lamb mince, breaking it up with the spoon, and stir in the cashews. Cook for 10 minutes, until nicely browned and completely cooked through, then stir in the fresh mint. Drain in a fine mesh sieve to remove all the excess oil and fat.

SALADS, SIDES AND SNACKS

ASSEMBLE AND COOK THE SAMOSAS

2 x 270g packs of filo pastry, thawed (or spring roll pastry if you can get it from an Asian market)

melted butter or ghee, for brushing the pastry (optional, if baking)

vegetable oil, for deep-frying (optional)

Preheat the oven to 210°C/190°C fan/gas 6 or heat the oil in a deep-fryer to 180°C (or see the tips on page 19 if you don't have a deep-fryer). Line two baking trays with non-stick baking paper.

To assemble, fill a small bowl with a little water for sealing the pastry. If you're baking the samosas you can brush one sheet of pastry with melted butter or ghee, place a second sheet directly on top and brush that with melted butter too if you like, but this isn't strictly necessary.

Working with two sheets of pastry at a time stacked neatly on top of each other, cut the pastry lengthways into three long rectangles. Keep the rest of the pastry on a plate under a damp clean tea towel or damp kitchen paper so that it doesn't dry out.

Put 1 tablespoon of the filling in the corner of the short edge of the rectangle closest to you. Take that corner of the pastry and fold it diagonally and up to the opposite side of the rectangle to form a triangle, then fold that triangle up and over itself to form another triangle. Repeat all the way up the rectangle until there is only one triangle (or portion of a triangle) left to fold.

Brush the last bit of pastry that you haven't folded yet with the water that you set aside in the bowl, then fold one last time, pinching a little to seal. Set aside on the lined baking trays and repeat with the rest of the pastry sheets and filling.

If you're baking the samosas in the oven, brush the tops with a little melted butter, then transfer the baking tray to the preheated oven and cook for about 20 minutes, until crisp and golden. If deep-frying, work in batches to deep-fry the samosas in the hot oil for 2–3 minutes on each side, until crisp and golden. Either way, drain the samosas briefly on a plate lined with kitchen paper to absorb any excess oil.

To serve *Serve while still warm with your favourite shop-bought mango chutney.*

SERVES **4** AS A SIDE

— SUBZ MILONI —
SUNIL'S STIR-FRIED VEGETABLES

In India, subz miloni is made totally differently to the way I make it. I developed this version as an easy vegetable option. It's essential that you have everything prepared and ready to go since it all cooks so quickly.

PREP

Measure out your spices into two separate small bowls: one bowl for the cumin seeds and one for the paprika, ground cumin, turmeric and salt.

Prep and measure out all the remaining ingredients before you start cooking so that everything is ready to go and the spices don't burn.

 ## COOK THE WHOLE SPICES

40ml vegetable oil

1 tsp cumin seeds

Heat the oil in a large frying pan over a high heat. Add the cumin seeds and cook for 1 minute, until fragrant.

 ## COOK THE BASE

30g cashews

30g raisins or sultanas

1 fresh red chilli, thinly sliced at an angle into rings

1½ tsp grated or finely chopped garlic

½ tsp paprika

¼ tsp ground cumin

¼ tsp ground turmeric

½ tsp fine sea salt

1 large ripe tomato, chopped

Add the cashews, raisins, red chilli and garlic and cook for 1 minute, then add the ground spices, salt, chopped tomato and **100ml water**. Let everything sizzle together for 1–2 minutes.

 ## STIR-FRY THE VEGETABLES

100g Tenderstem® broccoli, thinly sliced at an angle

100g fine green beans, thinly sliced at an angle

½ small courgette, thinly sliced at an angle (80g)

60g mangetout, thinly sliced at an angle

60g asparagus, woody ends snapped off and discarded, then thinly sliced at an angle

10 button mushrooms, quartered or sliced

Add all the vegetables and toss to coat in the sauce. Cook, stirring or tossing constantly, for just a few minutes so that the vegetables are heated through. I always prefer to undercook my vegetables slightly so that they still have plenty of freshness and crunch.

 ## TO FINISH

6 cherry tomatoes, halved

large handful of baby spinach

handful of fresh basil leaves

pinch of caster sugar

Add the cherry tomatoes, baby spinach, basil and a pinch of sugar and cook just until the spinach has lightly wilted. Serve immediately.

SERVES **4** AS A SIDE

— ALOO PHALI —
POTATOES AND FINE BEANS

We use fine green beans for this in Ireland since that's what is available, but in India we'd use a type called gawar phali, which are long and flat and naturally add a little sourness when cooked. I've recreated this by adding a handful of cherry tomatoes. At home in India this is eaten with chapati as a quick, inexpensive lunch.

PREP

Measure out your spices into two separate small bowls: one bowl for the cumin seeds and one for the ground turmeric.

Prep and measure out all the remaining ingredients before you start cooking so that everything is ready to go and the spices don't burn.

COOK THE WHOLE SPICES

40ml vegetable oil

1 tsp cumin seeds

Heat the oil in a large frying pan over a medium heat. Add the cumin seeds and cook for 1 minute, until fragrant.

COOK THE BEANS AND POTATOES

50g finely diced red onion or shallot

1 tbsp grated or finely chopped fresh ginger

1 fresh green chilli, halved lengthways

½ tsp fine sea salt

2 medium Rooster potatoes, peeled and cut into small dice

400g fine green beans, cut into quarters

¼ tsp ground turmeric

6 cherry tomatoes, halved

1–2 fresh thyme sprigs, leaves stripped

Add the onion or shallot, ginger, green chilli and salt and cook for about 5 minutes, until the onion has softened, then add the diced potatoes and stir to combine. Cover the pan, reduce the heat and cook for 5–10 minutes more, stirring once or twice, until the potatoes are just half-cooked.

Add the beans and turmeric, scraping the bottom of the pan, then add the cherry tomatoes and thyme leaves. Cover the pan again and leave for 2–3 minutes, until the beans are cooked but still have some bite and the potatoes are cooked through.

Serve straightaway, while the beans are still crisp and bright green.

180   SPICE BOX

SERVES **4** AS A SIDE

— CHONKA LAHSOONI PATTA —
BABY SPINACH WITH GARLIC AND FENNEL

This couldn't be simpler or quicker, but there is one trick: don't sprinkle salt directly on the spinach leaves, as it will just sit on them and won't get evenly distributed.

PREP

Prep and measure out all the remaining ingredients before you start cooking so that everything is ready to go and the spices don't burn.

30g butter

6 cherry tomatoes, halved

3–4 garlic cloves, chopped

1 tsp fennel seeds, ground in a pestle and mortar

½ tsp fine sea salt

200g baby spinach (or chard leaves or a mix of the two)

Melt the butter in a large frying pan over a low heat. Add the tomatoes, garlic, ground fennel and salt and cook for only 1 minute – you want the flavour of the garlic to stay strong in this dish.

Add the spinach and toss for just 20 seconds, just to gently warm but not wilt the leaves. Immediately transfer to a bowl and serve while still warm.

SPICE BOX

SERVES **2** TO **4** AS A SIDE

— JEERA ALOO —
POTATOES WITH CUMIN AND FRESH CORIANDER

My mother always made poori (page 205), this jeera aloo and mango pickle when we went on long train journeys, as they keep – and therefore travel – well.

> **PREP**
>
> Measure out your spices into two separate small bowls: one bowl for the cumin seeds and one for the ground cumin, turmeric, paprika and salt.
>
> Prep and measure out all the remaining ingredients before you start cooking so that everything is ready to go and the spices don't burn.

COOK THE POTATOES

2–3 large Rooster potatoes, peeled (500g cooked weight)

Boil the whole potatoes for about 15 minutes, until soft and completely cooked through. When they are cool enough to handle, cut into bite-sized pieces. You should have 500g of cooked, diced potato.

COOK THE WHOLE SPICES

50ml vegetable oil

1 tsp cumin seeds

Heat the oil in a large frying pan over a medium heat. Add the cumin seeds and cook for 1 minute, until fragrant.

BRING IT ALL TOGETHER

1 fresh green chilli, finely diced

1 tbsp grated or finely chopped fresh ginger

½ tsp ground cumin

½ tsp ground turmeric

¼ tsp paprika

½ tsp fine sea salt

Add the green chilli and ginger and cook for 1 minute before adding the diced potato and tossing together.

Add the ground spices and salt, then stir in **2 tablespoons water** so that the spices don't burn. Stir to coat the potatoes in all the spices and continue to cook, tossing occasionally, until the potatoes are heated through.

To serve *Sprinkle over some chopped fresh coriander and squeeze in some lemon juice.*

SALADS, SIDES AND SNACKS

SERVES **4** AS A SIDE

— ADRAKI GOBHI —
CAULIFLOWER WITH TURMERIC AND GINGER

Cauliflower is always served with something else in India, never on its own, but I wanted to showcase this vegetable and highlight how tasty it can be. I make this in a hot, dry wok in the restaurants to give it that nice roasted flavour.

PREP

Measure out your spices into three separate small bowls: one bowl for the fennel seeds and ginger matchsticks; one for the ground turmeric, cumin and salt; and one for the garam masala to finish.

Prep and measure out all the remaining ingredients before you start cooking so that everything is ready to go and the spices don't burn.

1 COOK THE WHOLE SPICES

40ml vegetable oil

1 tsp fennel seeds

thumb-sized piece of fresh ginger, cut into matchsticks

Heat the oil in a large heavy-based saucepan or wok over a medium heat. Add the fennel seeds and ginger and cook for 1 minute, until fragrant.

2 COOK THE CAULIFLOWER

1 head of cauliflower, cut into florets

2 fresh green chillies, halved lengthways

1 tsp ground turmeric

1 tsp ground cumin

1 tsp fine sea salt

Add the cauliflower florets, green chillies, turmeric, cumin, salt and **80ml water**, stirring to coat the cauliflower in the spices. Cover the pan or wok, reduce the heat to medium-low and simmer for 10–15 minutes, stirring occasionally, until the cauliflower is lightly charred around the edges and is soft but not mushy.

3 TO FINISH

1 small ripe tomato, chopped

1 tbsp chopped fresh coriander, plus extra to garnish

pinch of garam masala

Add the tomato, fresh coriander and garam masala. Cook for just 1 minute to bring everything together, then tip into a bowl, garnish with a little more coriander and serve hot.

SERVES **4** AS A SIDE

— GOATS' CHEESE TIKKI —
GOATS' CHEESE CAKES

I wanted to create a dish using a local goats' cheese on my menu after I had this dish at Benares in London; this is my own interpretation of it. It was tricky to get the balance of flavours just right – we even tried it with a grape chutney, but goats' cheese with pears and walnuts is a classic flavour combination that always tastes good together. It's like all the elements of a cheeseboard – cheese, pears, walnuts – put together into the cakes and chutney.

PREP

Measure out your spices into two separate small bowls: one bowl for the fennel and cumin seeds and one for the fenugreek and chilli flakes.

Prep and measure out all the remaining ingredients before you start cooking so that everything is ready to go and the spices don't burn.

MAKE THE SPICED OIL

70ml vegetable oil, plus extra for frying

1½ tsp fennel seeds

1 tsp cumin seeds

100g finely diced shallots

1 tsp fine sea salt

1 tbsp grated or finely chopped fresh ginger

1 tbsp finely chopped fresh chives

1 tbsp finely chopped fresh coriander stems

Heat the oil in a large frying pan over a medium heat. Add the fennel and cumin seeds and cook for 1 minute, until fragrant.

Remove the pan from the heat and add the shallots and salt, stirring to coat in the oil. Return the pan to a low heat and cook, stirring, for about 5 minutes. It's important not to brown the shallots here, just soften them. Add the ginger and cook for 1 minute.

Remove the pan from the heat again and stir in the fresh chives and coriander stems. Set aside to cool, then strain through a fine-mesh sieve, pressing the shallot mixture with the back of the spoon to extract as much flavour as possible into the oil.

186   SPICE BOX

MAKE THE GOATS' CHEESE CAKES

250g peeled, boiled and grated Rooster potato

200g chevre goats' cheese

1 tbsp chopped fresh coriander leaves, plus extra to garnish

1 tsp dried fenugreek leaves

pinch of chilli flakes

Put the cooked potato and goats' cheese in a bowl, then add the strained oil, chopped fresh coriander leaves, dried fenugreek leaves and chilli flakes. There's an art to mixing these cakes together – the key is to rub the mixture lightly, using your fingertips to gently combine everything together, almost as if you were rubbing butter into a pastry dough, lightly crumbling up the goats' cheese as you do. You're looking for a crumble-type consistency, not a paste.

Break off a generous portion of the mixture and roll it into a ball, then flatten down into a cake. Place on a plate and repeat with the rest of the mixture, then chill in the fridge for at least 30 minutes to firm up.

COOK THE CAKES

Heat a small drizzle of oil in a large non-stick frying pan over a low heat. Add the chilled goats' cheese cakes to the pan and cook for up to 5 minutes on each side, without moving them in the pan, until the bottom has turned golden brown and crisp but the cheese hasn't started to melt out of the cake. Carefully turn over and cook for a few minutes more.

To serve *The key to success with this recipe is to serve the cakes as soon as they come off the pan, otherwise they can start to flatten out on the plate. Serve the goats' cheese cakes with a few spoonfuls of pear and walnut chutney (page 234) on the side and garnish with a little chopped fresh coriander.*

SERVES **4** TO **6** AS A SIDE

— MAKAI KHUMBH BADAM KI SUBZI —
WILD MUSHROOMS AND SWEETCORN WITH ALMONDS

In India we don't have as many different types of mushrooms as you can get here in Ireland, so the first time I heard the term 'wild mushrooms', I didn't understand and thought they were poisonous, even though there is a tradition of foraging for mushrooms and morels in Himachal. Almonds are a staple Himachali food, so it makes sense to use them here. Serve this as a side to a lamb or chicken curry (but not a korma) or as a samosa filling.

PREP

Measure out your spices into two separate small bowls: one for the ground coriander and one for the paprika to finish.

Prep and measure out all the remaining ingredients before you start cooking so that everything is ready to go and the spices don't burn.

COOK THE WHOLE SPICES

1 tbsp vegetable oil

1–2 cloves, crushed with a rolling pin

Heat the oil in a large frying pan or wok over a medium heat. Add the crushed cloves and cook for 1 minute, until fragrant.

190   SPICE BOX

 ## COOK THE VEGETABLES

1 medium red onion,
thinly sliced

1 tsp fine sea salt

2–3 fresh green chillies,
halved lengthways

1 tbsp grated or finely
chopped garlic

400g mixed wild
mushrooms, sliced

150g sweetcorn

80g flaked almonds

1 tsp ground coriander

2 knobs of butter or
ghee

Add the onion and salt and cook for 5 minutes, until softened. Add the green chillies and garlic and cook for 1 minute, until fragrant.

Raise the heat as high as it will go, then add the mushrooms and cook, stirring or tossing constantly, for 3–4 minutes. You should always cook mushrooms over a high heat without any water to get the best flavour out of them.

Add the sweetcorn, flaked almonds and ground coriander and cook for a few minutes more, still stirring or tossing constantly over a high heat as if it were a stir-fry.

Make an open space in the centre of the pan, then add the butter or ghee and allow it to melt before tossing to coat the vegetables in it.

 ## TO FINISH

6 cherry tomatoes,
halved

½ tsp paprika

15g fresh basil

Add the cherry tomatoes and paprika and cook for 1–2 minutes to bring everything together, then tear in the fresh basil leaves.

SERVES **4**

— KHATTA MEETHA KADDU —
SWEET-AND-SOUR PUMPKIN

This is a dish from northern India, where pumpkin is often served with poori in restaurants and where it's eaten once a week when it's in season. I used to serve this with venison and a cranberry chutney at Pickle and it was a spectacular combination. Don't use the bright orange pumpkins that you carve at Halloween – look for the crown prince or kabocha varieties, or failing that, use a butternut squash instead.

PREP

Measure out your spices into two separate small bowls: one bowl for the whole spices and one for the ground coriander, paprika, cumin, turmeric and ginger.

Prep and measure out all the remaining ingredients before you start cooking so that everything is ready to go and the spices don't burn.

1 COOK THE WHOLE SPICES

60ml strong-flavoured rapeseed oil

1 tsp fennel seeds

1 tsp nigella seeds

½ tsp cumin seeds

½ tsp coriander seeds

Heat the oil in a large heavy-based saucepan over a medium heat. Add the fennel, nigella, cumin and coriander seeds and cook for 1 minute, until fragrant.

2 COOK THE PUMPKIN

½ small red onion, finely diced (80g)

½ tsp fine sea salt

1 tbsp grated or finely chopped fresh ginger

1 tbsp ground coriander

1½ tsp paprika

½ tsp ground cumin

½ tsp ground turmeric

½ tsp ground ginger

1 pumpkin or butternut squash, peeled and diced (600g)

1 tbsp dark brown sugar

25ml apple cider vinegar

Add the onion and salt and cook for about 5 minutes, until softened. Add the ginger and cook for 1 minute more.

Add the ground spices and **100ml water** so that the spices don't burn. Cook for 1 minute, then add the pumpkin or squash, stirring to coat in all the spices. Cover the pan, reduce the heat a little and cook for 10–15 minutes, until the pumpkin or squash is soft. Stir once or twice to make sure nothing is catching and burning on the bottom of the pan.

Add the brown sugar, apple cider vinegar, **1 tablespoon of water** and ¼ teaspoon of salt (or to taste). Simmer for a few minutes more, uncovered, until nice and thick.

3 TO FINISH

large handful of chopped fresh coriander (optional)

Garnish with a large handful of chopped fresh coriander (if using).

To serve *Serve with naan (shop-bought or page 211), Sunil's garlic bread (page 218), roti (page 214) or aloo paratha (page 216).*

SALADS, SIDES AND SNACKS

SERVES **4** AS A SIDE

— BAINGAN BHARTA —
PUNJABI AUBERGINE MASH

Twenty years ago, aubergines were treated like gold in Indian restaurants – they were more expensive than chicken. This dish is done differently in different regions. For example, baingan ka chokha is a version where the aubergine is charred, but everything else is left raw (a similar dish called aloo chokha is made with potatoes that are cooked in the smouldering ashes of the fire in a chulha clay stove). This is the smoky, spicy Punjabi version.

PREP

Measure out your spices into two separate small bowls: one bowl for the cumin seeds and one for the ground coriander, cumin, paprika and turmeric.

Prep and measure out all the remaining ingredients before you start cooking so that everything is ready to go and the spices don't burn.

COOK THE AUBERGINES

2 aubergines, skin scored

Lightly grease the aubergines all over with a little oil, then place directly on the gas flame of your hob or on a ridged griddle pan. Cook until the aubergines have softened and collapsed. When they're cool enough to handle, peel off all the charred skin using your hands, not a peeler. Finely chop the flesh until it's practically broken down to a purée.

COOK THE WHOLE SPICES

70ml vegetable oil, plus extra for greasing

1½ tsp cumin seeds

Heat the oil in a large heavy-based saucepan over a medium heat. Add the cumin seeds and cook for 1 minute, until fragrant.

SPICE BOX

MAKE THE MASH

1 large onion, finely diced

1 tsp fine sea salt

3–4 green chillies, chopped

1 tbsp grated or finely chopped fresh ginger

1 tbsp grated or finely chopped garlic

1½ tbsp ground coriander

2 tsp ground cumin

1½ tsp paprika

1 tsp ground turmeric

3 ripe tomatoes, chopped

Add the onion and salt to the pan and cook for about 10 minutes, stirring occasionally, until softened but only lightly browned. Add the green chillies, ginger and garlic and cook for 1 minute more.

Add the ground spices and cook for 1 minute before adding the tomatoes. Cook for 5 minutes to soften and break down the tomatoes, then stir in the aubergine flesh and cook, stirring, for a few minutes more to bring the flavours together.

TO FINISH

¼ tsp fine sea salt

2 tbsp chopped fresh coriander

pinch of garam masala

Season with ¼ teaspoon of salt (or to taste), then add the fresh coriander and a pinch of garam masala. Serve hot.

SALADS, SIDES AND SNACKS

SERVES **4** AS A SIDE

— ASPARAGUS PORIYAL —
ASPARAGUS WITH COCONUT AND MUSTARD SEEDS

This simple dish literally takes only minutes to make. I used to make something similar using fine green beans since asparagus isn't an ingredient used in traditional Indian cuisine, but I like to use the produce that is available here in Ireland. Try this with chard leaves, broccoli or kale instead of asparagus.

PREP

Measure out your spices into two separate bowls: one small bowl for the whole spices and one medium bowl for the pinch of turmeric and paprika.

Prep and measure out all the remaining ingredients before you start cooking so that everything is ready to go and the spices don't burn.

PREPARE THE ASPARAGUS

1 bunch of asparagus

Snap off the woody ends of each asparagus spear where it naturally breaks, then slice the asparagus sharply on the diagonal.

COOK THE WHOLE SPICES

1 tbsp vegetable oil

1 fresh or dried red chilli, halved lengthways

½ tsp mustard seeds

Heat the oil in a large frying pan or wok over a medium heat. Add the red chilli and mustard seeds and cook for 1 minute, until the seeds start to pop. Mustard seeds can burn and turn bitter very quickly, so watch them carefully.

BRING IT ALL TOGETHER

½ small red onion, finely diced

½ tsp fine sea salt

2 large garlic cloves, grated or finely chopped

1 tsp grated or finely chopped fresh ginger

2 tbsp desiccated coconut

small pinch of turmeric

small pinch of paprika

knob of butter or ghee

Add the onion and salt and cook for 3 minutes, stirring, then add the garlic and ginger and cook for 1 minute more before adding the asparagus, coconut and a pinch of turmeric and paprika. Reduce the heat, add the butter or ghee and cook, tossing constantly, for just 2 minutes.

Serve straightaway, while the asparagus is still crisp and bright green.

SALADS, SIDES AND SNACKS

SERVES **4** AS A SIDE

— ḤARI GOBI SHIMLA MIRCH —
BROCCOLI AND PEPPERS WITH PUMPKIN SEEDS

Whenever I'd go to an Avoca café, I'd see their famous broccoli, tomato, feta and hazelnut salad. Broccoli isn't associated with Indian cuisine, so I was inspired by them to create a fresh dish of my own for Street. It needs to be served straightaway to keep its texture and colour.

PREP

Measure out your spices into two separate small bowls: one bowl for all the seeds and one for the ground coriander, fennel and salt.

Prep and measure out all the remaining ingredients before you start cooking so that everything is ready to go and the spices don't burn.

1 COOK THE SEEDS

2 tbsp strong-flavoured rapeseed oil

40g pumpkin seeds

2 tsp fennel seeds

1 tsp coriander seeds

Heat the oil in a large heavy-based frying pan or saucepan over a medium heat. Add the pumpkin, fennel and coriander seeds and cook for 1 minute, until fragrant.

2 COOK THE BROCCOLI AND PEPPER

1 large head of broccoli, broken into florets (400g florets)

1 red, green or yellow pepper, roughly chopped (150g)

2 tbsp grated or finely chopped fresh ginger

1 tbsp ground coriander

2 tsp fennel seeds, ground in a pestle and mortar

½ tsp fine sea salt

Add the broccoli and cook for 1 minute, tossing to coat in the oil and seeds. Add the chopped pepper and the ginger and cook for 1 minute more before adding the ground spices, salt and **60ml water**. Cover the pan with a lid and cook for 5 minutes – you want the broccoli and peppers to keep their bright colours and some crunch.

3 TO FINISH

150g cherry tomatoes, halved

1 tbsp chopped fresh coriander

1 lemon wedge

Add the cherry tomatoes and chopped fresh coriander and squeeze in the lemon juice. Cook for just 1 minute to bring everything together, then serve straightaway.

SERVES **4**

— SAUNF SEV KA SALAAD —
APPLE AND FENNEL SALAD

This isn't a traditional Indian dish, but I love how simple and elegant this salad is. I like to serve it with the pan-fried mackerel on page 122, but it would be nice with so many things. I learned this from Chef Sameer Miglani in India, who had recently taken over and was putting his own stamp on the menu. He had just come back from working in Melbourne, where he learned this recipe, and he was adamant about putting it on the menu at the Oberoi Group. He insisted that the apple and fennel were shaved so thinly that you could see through them. He loved this salad and I love it too.

MAKE THE DRESSING

2 tbsp pine nuts

1½ tsp grated or finely chopped garlic

zest and juice of 1 lemon

50ml olive oil

½ tsp fine sea salt

freshly ground black pepper

First make the dressing. Lightly crush the pine nuts with the back of a wooden spoon or a rolling pin to add a little body to the dressing. Put in a bowl with all the other dressing ingredients, including the reserved fennel fronds, and whisk together.

MAKE THE SALAD

1 fennel bulb, halved (keep the fronds for the dressing)

1 Pink Lady apple, halved and cored

Bring a small saucepan of water to the boil. Add the fennel and blanch it for only 10 seconds – you just want to soften it a little but not lose all its crunch. Transfer to a bowl of iced water to stop it cooking any further.

Use a mandoline to shave the apple as thinly as possible, but if you don't have a mandoline, you could use the thinnest slicing disc on your food processor or a sharp knife and a steady hand. Put in a large bowl.

Drain the fennel in a colander, then squeeze it firmly to get rid of as much water as possible. Shave it as thinly as possible too, then add to the bowl with the apple and mix gently to coat in the dressing.

To serve *Add a small mound of the salad to each plate and garnish with freshly ground pink peppercorns.*

SALADS, SIDES AND SNACKS   199

SERVES **6**

— SIRKA PYAZ —
PICKLED RED ONIONS

It's best to leave this to pickle overnight in the fridge to let the flavour and bright pink colour develop, but we leave it for two days before using it in the restaurants. I serve this with the tandoori-style chicken on page 42 and the chickpea curry on page 136.

50ml distilled or white wine vinegar

4 tsp caster sugar

1 tsp fine sea salt

1 large red onion, cut in half from the root to the tip (200g)

1 small beetroot, cut into matchsticks

Put the vinegar, sugar and salt in a medium glass bowl and whisk to combine.

Having cut your onion in half from the root to the tip (rather than around its middle) and still working lengthways from the root end to the tip, cut it into very thin slices. This way, you'll get more even, consistent slices for your pickle.

Add the onion and beetroot to the bowl and gently toss everything together. Cover the bowl with cling film and leave it in the fridge overnight. The next day, the onion and beetroot will have softened and everything will be bright pink.

This will keep for up to a month in a sealed jar in the fridge.

RICE AND BREAD

★

CHAPTER 6

SERVES **6**

— SAFED CHAWAL —
PLAIN BOILED BASMATI RICE

People always ask me how to make rice to get perfectly cooked, fluffy rice every time – my trick is to add a little oil to the cooking water. My method is similar to the way you cook pasta – in plenty of boiling salted water – and is one of the most foolproof ways of getting separate grains of rice. Tilda is a good brand, but the main thing is that you use basmati rice, not a different variety.

This recipe is for plain rice, but you could add any number of other things to the pan while the rice is cooking to add a hint of flavour and a bit of scent, such as the juice and squeezed-out halves of one lemon; star anise, cumin seeds and a cinnamon stick, which is my favourite; or a pinch of fenugreek seeds for a nice flavour and to aid digestion, which is what my mother does.

RINSE AND SOAK THE RICE

500g basmati rice

Rinse the rice a few times in a big bowl of water, being careful not to break the grains as basmati rice is very delicate and broken grains will release starch, which you don't want. After rinsing, leave the rice to soak for 30 minutes, then drain. Rinsing the rice like this gets rid of any impurities and soaking it is key to getting those fluffy, separate grains.

COOK THE RICE

1½ tbsp fine sea salt

1 tbsp vegetable oil

Bring **3 litres water** and the salt to the boil in a large saucepan. Add the oil, then add the drained rice and stir gently from the bottom. With the heat still on high, cook, uncovered, for just 5 minutes. Check a few grains of rice – it should be soft enough to easily crush it between your fingers. It should be almost cooked but still have a little bite, like cooking pasta until it's al dente. The longer you soaked the rice for, the less time it will take to cook. Cook it for a few minutes more only if it really needs it – don't overcook or your rice will be mushy, not fluffy.

Drain the rice, then return it to the pan off the heat, cover and leave to stand for a few minutes. Fluff up with a fork to separate the grains before serving.

204   SPICE BOX

MAKES ABOUT **16**

— POORI —

These deep-fried breads will puff up like a balloon when you cook them and are either eaten with a curry, like the chickpea curry on page 136 or the potato curry on page 134, or on their own as a snack.

MAKE THE DOUGH

500g fine wholemeal flour (or chapati flour if you can get it)

50g semolina (optional, for extra texture)

½ tsp fine sea salt

1 tbsp vegetable oil

Mix the flour, semolina (if using) and salt together in a large bowl, then pour in **300ml water** and the oil. Use your hands or a stand mixer fitted with a dough hook to knead together into a firm dough – this will take anywhere between 5 and 10 minutes and you may need an extra splash of water to help it come together.

Cover with a clean, damp tea towel and set aside to rest in a warm place for at least 20 minutes, but the longer you can leave it, the better. The dough will be very stiff and tight at first, but once it has rested it will have relaxed to the perfect texture and will be easy to work with, so don't be tempted to add more liquid unless you really need it.

COOK THE POORI

vegetable oil, for deep-frying

Heat the oil in a deep-fryer to 200°C (or 190°C if your fryer doesn't go that high). Make sure the oil is really hot before you start cooking – if it isn't, you'll never get good poori. Alternatively, see the tips on page 19 if you don't have a deep-fryer.

Tip the dough out on to the work surface and briefly knead. Break off a 30g portion, roll into a ball and press down to flatten, then use a rolling pin to roll out until it's about 10cm across. You want the dough to be rolled out thinly but not too thin – you don't want the bread to crisp up like a poppadum.

Working with one dough circle at a time, deep-fry the poori in the hot oil until they are puffed up and light golden on both sides, using tongs to turn them over. Drain on a baking tray lined with kitchen paper to absorb any excess oil.

Make sure the oil has come back up to temperature before you cook the next one. Serve warm.

RICE AND BREAD

SERVES **6**

— NIMBU WALE CHAWAL —
LEMON RICE

Lemon rice has so much flavour that you can eat it on its own or with any fish curry – or even as a one-pot breakfast, like we do in India. This dish comes from Kerala, in southern India, where it complements the flavour profile of the dishes from that region. This is often made to use up leftover rice and leftover split peas or lentils to turn them into a new dish. If you're allergic to peanuts, use almonds or cashews instead.

PREP

Measure out your spices into two separate small bowls: one bowl for the yellow split peas, red chillies and mustard seeds; and one for the turmeric.

Prep and measure out all the remaining ingredients before you start cooking so that everything is ready to go and the spices don't burn.

 ## COOK THE RICE

400g basmati rice
(or 1kg cooked rice)

Cook the rice as per the recipe for plain boiled basmati rice on page 204.

 ## COOK THE SPICES

50ml vegetable oil

30g dried yellow
split peas

2 fresh or dried red
chillies, chopped

1 tsp mustard seeds

Heat the oil in a large heavy-based saucepan over a medium heat. Add the yellow split peas and cook for 1 minute, then add the red chillies and mustard seeds and cook for 1 minute more, until the mustard seeds start to pop.

 ## BRING IT ALL TOGETHER

1 small red onion, finely
chopped

1 tsp fine sea salt

1 fresh green chilli,
finely chopped

1 tbsp grated or finely
chopped fresh ginger

50g red-skinned
peanuts

10g fresh coriander,
chopped

juice of 1 large lemon
(50ml)

1 tsp ground turmeric

Add the onion and salt and cook for 5–8 minutes, until the onion is softened but not browned. Add the green chilli and ginger and cook for 1 minute, until fragrant, then add the peanuts, chopped fresh coriander, lemon juice and turmeric before stirring in the cooked rice. Cook, stirring, for a few minutes, until the rice is thoroughly reheated.

 ## TO FINISH

fresh coconut shavings
or dried coconut flakes
(optional)

Scatter over fresh or dried coconut (if using) and serve hot.

SERVES **6** TO **8**

— PULAO —
SPICED BASMATI RICE WITH PEAS AND RED ONION

As with the plain boiled basmati rice on page 204, you could add just about any spices, fresh herbs or aromatics that you like to this recipe instead of the peas, red onion and spices I've used here, so experiment with this recipe to make it your own. I remember sitting on the couch with all four of my siblings, all of us eating bowls of pulao that my mother had made using potatoes, onions, cumin seeds and turmeric.

PREP

Measure out your whole spices into a small bowl.

Prep and measure out all the remaining ingredients before you start cooking so that everything is ready to go and the spices don't burn.

1 RINSE AND SOAK THE RICE

500g basmati rice

Rinse the rice a few times in a big bowl of water, being careful not to break the grains as basmati rice is very delicate and broken grains will release starch, which you don't want. After rinsing, leave the rice to soak for 30 minutes, then drain. Rinsing the rice like this gets rid of any impurities and soaking it is key to getting those fluffy, separate grains.

2 COOK THE SPICES

40g butter or ghee
4 green cardamom pods
4 cloves
2 bay leaves
1 cinnamon stick
1 star anise
½ tsp cumin seeds

Melt the butter or ghee in a large heavy-based saucepan. Add the cardamom pods, cloves, bay leaves, cinnamon stick, star anise and cumin seeds and cook for 1 minute, until fragrant.

3 MAKE THE PULAO

1 red onion, thinly sliced
1 fresh green chilli, finely chopped
1 tsp fine sea salt
200g frozen petits pois
1 ripe tomato, left whole
large knob of butter

Add the red onion, green chilli and salt and cook for 5–8 minutes, until the onion is softened but not browned. Add the drained rice, peas and **1 litre water**, then nestle the tomato in the centre of the pan and bring to the boil. When the water is starting to get absorbed after a few minutes, dot the butter on top without stirring it in.

Reduce the heat to its lowest setting and press a piece of parchment paper directly on top of the rice, then cover with a tight-fitting lid. Cook for 10 minutes without lifting the lid.

Check the rice after 10 minutes – all the water should have been absorbed and the rice should be cooked, but if not, cover the pan and cook for a few minutes more. When the rice is done, stir to combine everything. It shouldn't stick to the bottom of the pan because of the butter that you added.

To serve *Transfer to a serving dish and fluff up with a fork, then scatter over a handful of shop-bought crispy onions.*

MAKES **6** TO **8**

– NAAN, THREE WAYS –

You can buy naan in any supermarket, but making homemade naan is so easy. I've given you three versions here: plain, chilli and cumin, and garlic and coriander. If making the chilli and cumin naan be sure to use whole spices, not ground, as they will burn in the hot oven. My father used to make naan on the walls of a pressure cooker, uncovered, to mimic cooking it in a tandoor.

MAKE THE BASIC DOUGH

1 x 7g sachet of fast-action dried yeast

1 tbsp caster sugar

200ml lukewarm water

500g plain flour, plus extra for dusting

1 tsp fine sea salt

50ml full-fat milk

1½ tsp vegetable oil

1 egg

Sprinkle the yeast and sugar on top of the lukewarm water, give it a quick stir and set aside for 10 minutes, until the yeast has activated and turned frothy.

Put the flour and salt in the bowl of a stand mixer fitted with a dough hook and mix together, then make a well in the centre. (You could also do this all by hand if you don't have a stand mixer.)

In a separate large jug, measure out the milk and vegetable oil. Crack in the egg and whisk to combine, then pour it into the well in the dry ingredients along with the yeast and water mixture.

Knead on a medium speed for 10 minutes to bring together into a soft, elastic dough. The dough will seem to be too dry at first, but keep kneading and it will come together. If not, drizzle in a teaspoon more water at a time as required. Cover with a clean tea towel and set aside to rest in a warm place for 1 hour, until doubled in size.

Preheat the oven to 260°C/240°C fan/gas 10, or as hot as it will go. Heat up a pizza stone or baking tray in the oven as it preheats too. You need to use the hottest temperature to get the naan nice and fluffy – the lower the temperature, the crispier the naan will be, which isn't what you want. It should be soft and pillowy.

Tip the dough out on to a clean work surface and briefly knead it again, then divide it evenly into six or eight portions.

RICE AND BREAD

② FOR PLAIN NAAN

large pinch of nigella seeds (optional)

melted butter, for brushing

Put a small pinch of nigella seeds on top of each ball of dough (if using) or leave them completely plain. Roll out each ball of dough until it's a thin circle or oval (roll the dough diagonally if you want ovals).

FOR CHILLI AND CUMIN NAAN

large pinch of red chilli flakes

large pinch of cumin seeds

large pinch of flaky sea salt

melted butter, for brushing

Combine the chilli flakes, cumin seeds and flaky sea salt in a small bowl. Dip the top of each ball of dough in this mixture before rolling it out into a thin circle or oval (roll the dough diagonally if you want ovals).

FOR GARLIC AND CORIANDER NAAN

50g butter or ghee

2–3 garlic cloves, finely chopped or crushed

1–2 tbsp finely chopped fresh coriander

large pinch of flaky sea salt

Roll out each ball of dough until it's a thin circle or oval (roll the dough diagonally if you want ovals). Put the butter and garlic in a small saucepan set over a medium heat and cook until the butter has melted and the garlic has softened and lost its raw pungency, but be careful not to let the garlic overcook or burn and turn bitter. Keep warm and set aside.

Or for a different taste and texture, I like to put the raw chopped garlic directly on top of the naan before baking it, then brushing it with plain butter after it comes out of the oven.

③ BAKE AND FINISH

Put the naan on two baking trays and cook in the preheated oven for 5 minutes, until puffed up and golden brown.

Remove from the oven and brush the plain or chilli and cumin naan with melted butter. If you're making the garlic and coriander naan, brush it with the garlic butter, then scatter over the chopped fresh coriander and some flaky sea salt. Serve warm.

MAKES **15**

— KHASTA ROTI —

Roti, which are Indian flatbreads, are usually cooked in a blazing-hot tandoor oven, but pan-frying works fine at home. I love to make a spiced version of these to eat with the Indian scrambled eggs on page 142 – after you've rolled it out, spread the roti all over with softened butter, then sprinkle over a pinch of paprika, ground cumin, salt and a small pinch of flour. Fold the dough in half and spread the top with more butter, then fold that in half again so that it's now a quarter circle. Roll out again to the size of a tortilla and cook as below.

MAKE THE DOUGH

500g fine wholemeal flour

½ tsp fine sea salt

Put the flour and salt in a large bowl and whisk together, then gradually pour in **300ml water** and mix to a dough. You can either do this by hand or in the bowl of a stand mixer fitted with the dough hook attachment. Cover the bowl with a clean tea towel and set it aside to rest for at least 30 minutes. The dough won't rise because there isn't any yeast in it, but it will relax and be easier to work with.

COOK AND FINISH

plenty of melted butter, for brushing

Break off 50g portions of dough and roll them out thinly – they should be about the size of a tortilla.

Heat a large, dry frying pan over a medium heat. Working with one at a time, add a roti and cook for 1 minute on each side until spotted all over and golden brown, pressing down on the roti with the spatula to prevent it puffing up and to keep it in contact with the hot pan. Keep flipping the roti over as many times as are needed so that it's cooked through and nicely charred. You might need to cook it two or three times on each side.

Brush the top of the roti with a little melted butter and slide it out of the pan on to a plate. Serve warm.

MAKES **15**

— ALOO PARATHA —
POTATO FLATBREADS

I'm obsessed with potatoes. Samosas, potato cakes, aloo paratha – I love them all. This is my absolute favourite breakfast served with fresh butter on top or yoghurt on the side and a big glass of lassi (pages 258 and 260). These flatbreads start off exactly the same as the roti recipe on page 214, but then get stuffed with a potato filling. Aloo paratha is like samosas – everyone loves it and it's served everywhere. All tea shops have stacks of paratha waiting to be slapped on to a hot griddle.

> **PREP**
>
> Measure out the cumin seeds, chilli flakes and salt for the stuffing into a small bowl.
>
> Prep and measure out all the remaining ingredients before you start cooking so that everything is ready to go and the spices don't burn.

COOK THE POTATOES

400g Maris Piper potatoes, peeled

First cook the potatoes in a saucepan of boiling lightly salted water for 15–20 minutes, until completely cooked through but not overcooked – a sharp knife should be able to slide through the potato easily. Drain and set aside until they are cool enough to handle, then grate with the large holes on a box grater. You should have about 250g of cooked, grated potato.

MAKE THE DOUGH

500g fine wholemeal flour

½ tsp fine sea salt

Meanwhile, put the flour and salt in a large bowl and whisk together, then gradually pour in **300ml water** and mix to a dough. You can either do this by hand or in the bowl of a stand mixer fitted with the dough hook attachment. Wrap up the dough in cling film and set it aside to rest for 30 minutes.

MAKE THE STUFFING

1 fresh green chilli, finely chopped

1 tsp grated or finely chopped fresh ginger

1 tbsp finely chopped fresh coriander

1 tsp toasted cumin seeds

½ tsp chilli flakes

½ tsp fine sea salt

Put the grated potato, green chilli, ginger, chopped fresh coriander, cumin seeds, chilli flakes and salt in a medium bowl and mix until evenly combined.

Break off 80g portions of the dough. Roll one into a ball and make a deep indent in the middle of it with your thumb. Stuff with 50g of the potato filling, then bring the dough around the filling to completely enclose it. Use your hands to press down the dough into a disc, then roll it out thinly but not too thin: aim for 5mm. Repeat with the remaining dough and filling.

COOK THE PARATHA

vegetable oil

Heat a dry frying pan over a medium-high heat. Working with one at a time, add one flatbread to the hot pan and cook for 2 minutes, until nicely charred all over. Flip over, drizzle a little oil on top and spread it around and cook for 1–2 minutes more, until the bread is cooked and the filling is heated through.

To serve Slide the aloo paratha out of the pan, add a small piece of butter on top and allow it to melt. Serve warm with thick Greek yoghurt.

MAKES **2** LONG BAGUETTES

– SUNIL'S GARLIC BREAD –

When we were opening an Oberoi hotel in Shimla, we did a lot of outdoor catering because the hotel had a lot of land. The kitchen would provide 10 different types of chutneys for the bar, where they would be served with garlic bread sliced very thinly and crisped up. Garlic bread is good with anything, but I love it with the sweet-and-sour aubergine chutney on page 226.

MAKE THE GARLIC BUTTER

150g salted butter, softened

1 small head of garlic, cloves peeled and finely chopped

1 tbsp chopped fresh coriander, thyme or parsley

1 tsp chilli flakes

Preheat the oven to 240°C/220°C fan/gas 9.

Mix the softened butter, garlic, chopped fresh herbs and chilli flakes in a medium bowl until evenly combined.

PREPARE THE BREAD

2 long baguettes or 1 extra-long baguette, cut in half

Cut each baguette into thin slices all down its length like a hasselback potato – in other words, cut it as if you were going to cut it into thin slices but without cutting all the way through the bottom of the bread. Spread the softened butter all over the top of the baguette, making sure to push it down in between all the slices.

BAKE THE BREAD

flaky sea salt

Wrap up the baguettes in foil and pop directly on to the middle shelf of the oven. Bake for 10–15 minutes to allow the butter to melt, then open up the foil and bake for 5–10 minutes more, until the top of the bread is golden. Sprinkle a pinch of flaky sea salt on top and serve warm.

CHAPTER 7

CHUTNEYS AND RAITAS

MAKES **800ML**

— BENGALI CHUTNEY —
TOMATO AND CASHEW CHUTNEY

This chutney is from the eastern side of India, around Bengal.

> **PREP**
>
> Measure out your spices into two separate small bowls: one bowl for the whole spices and one for the sugar, paprika and salt.
>
> Prep and measure out all the remaining ingredients before you start cooking so that everything is ready to go and the spices don't burn.

COOK THE WHOLE SPICES

50ml vegetable oil

2–3 fresh or dried red chillies, halved lengthways

2–3 bay leaves

1 cinnamon stick

2 tsp nigella seeds

1½ tsp fennel seeds

Heat the oil in a large saucepan over a medium heat. Add the red chillies, bay leaves, cinnamon stick, nigella seeds and fennel seeds and cook for 1 minute, until fragrant.

MAKE THE CHUTNEY

75g cashews

750g vine-ripened tomatoes, halved and sliced

100g sultanas

½ tsp ground cinnamon

350ml white wine vinegar

300g caster sugar

3 tbsp paprika

2 tbsp fine sea salt

juice of ½ lemon

Add the cashews and cook for 2 minutes, then add the tomatoes, sultanas and ground cinnamon and cook for 3 minutes more before stirring in the vinegar, sugar, paprika and salt. Bring to the boil, then reduce the heat and simmer for 20–30 minutes, until the tomatoes have broken down and the chutney has reduced to a thick, jammy texture. Stir in the lemon juice at the end to keep its sharp flavour.

Spoon into a clean jar and store in the fridge, where it will keep for months.

MAKES **400ML**

— DHANIYA PUDINA KI CHUTNEY —
MINT AND CORIANDER CHUTNEY

This chutney is the freshest thing you can eat – it brightens up just about anything. You'll find this chutney everywhere in India, but a lot of places often don't use the right proportion of mint and coriander. My mother would never use a blender when making this, but rather would pound it by hand in a pestle and mortar. It makes a lot, but you can cut the amounts in half if you don't need quite so much.

1 green apple, skin on, cored and roughly chopped

4 small fresh green chillies, roughly chopped

juice of 2 lemons

3 tbsp olive oil

1 tsp fine sea salt

½ tsp caster sugar

3–4 ice cubes

70g fresh mint (leaves and stems if they aren't tough or woody)

50g fresh coriander (leaves and stems)

Put the apple, green chillies, lemon juice, olive oil, salt, sugar and ice cubes in a blender and blitz until combined. The ice is needed to counteract the heat from the blades of the food processor or blender, which would discolour the fresh herbs and make your chutney turn black instead of the vibrant green it should be.

Add the fresh mint and coriander and blend again. You may need to add more oil or ice cubes to get it to blend and combine.

Transfer to a clean jar and store in the fridge for 1–2 days.

MAKES **550G**

— BAINGAN CHUTNEY —
SWEET-AND-SOUR AUBERGINE CHUTNEY

Lyn Middlehurst, who founded and writes the Gallivanter's Guide in the UK, would often come to India to rate the Oberoi hotels. We always knew in advance that she would be coming, so Chef Gulshan, our executive chef, wanted to create something special for her. He put a small jar of this chutney in her room and she liked it so much, she asked if she could have a 1kg jar to take home with her. I love this chutney spread on my garlic bread (page 218) – heaven on Earth.

PREP

Measure out your spices into two separate small bowls: one for the whole spices and one for the sugar, ground coriander, paprika, cumin and garam masala.

Prep and measure out all the remaining ingredients before you start cooking so that everything is ready to go and the spices don't burn.

FRY THE AUBERGINES

2 aubergines, cut into thick matchsticks

1–2 tsp fine sea salt, for sprinkling over

vegetable oil, for deep-frying

Spread the aubergine matchsticks evenly over a baking tray, then sprinkle with salt. Leave for 30 minutes to allow the salt to draw out the bitter juices from the aubergine, then drain in a colander and squeeze out as much water as possible.

Heat some vegetable oil in a deep-fryer to 190°C (or see the tips on page 19 if you don't have a deep-fryer). Working in batches so that you don't crowd the fryer, fry the aubergine for 5 minutes, until deep golden brown and crisp. Transfer to a plate lined with kitchen paper to absorb any excess oil and set aside.

COOK THE WHOLE SPICES

50ml vegetable oil

2–3 bay leaves

1 fresh or dried red chilli, chopped

1 tsp cumin seeds

1 tsp coriander seeds

1 tsp mustard seeds

1 tsp fennel seeds

Heat the oil in a large heavy-based saucepan over a medium heat. Add the bay leaves, red chilli and seeds and cook for 1 minute, until fragrant.

MAKE THE CHUTNEY

1 small red onion, finely diced

1½ tsp fine sea salt

2 tbsp grated or finely chopped fresh ginger

2 tbsp grated or finely chopped garlic

2½ tbsp caster sugar

1 tbsp ground coriander

1 tbsp paprika

1 tsp ground cumin

½ tsp garam masala

60ml white wine vinegar

70g tomato purée

Add the onion and salt and cook for just a few minutes – you want the onion to still have some crunch to it. Add the ginger and garlic and cook for 1 minute more.

Add the sugar, ground spices and vinegar and allow to bubble up for 1 minute, then add the tomato purée and **a splash of water** to bring everything together. Cook for 10 minutes to allow the flavours to combine.

TO FINISH

1 tbsp chopped fresh coriander

Gently fold in the deep-fried aubergine and chopped fresh coriander, but try not to overmix so that you don't break up the aubergine matchsticks too much.

This will keep in a sealed jar or airtight container in the fridge for up to a week.

SERVES 4

— SOYA PATTA RAITA —
DILL RAITA

Raita = rai (mustard) and ta (yoghurt). If you blend yoghurt and freshly ground mustard seeds into a paste and leave them overnight, it turns the yoghurt sour. My version of dill raita is a golden yellow colour from the turmeric.

PREP

Measure out your whole spices into a small bowl.

Prep and measure out all the remaining ingredients before you start cooking so that everything is ready to go.

COOK THE WHOLE SPICES

½ tbsp vegetable oil

1 fresh or dried red chilli, halved lengthways

½ tsp mustard seeds

½ tsp ground turmeric

Heat the oil in a small frying pan over a medium heat. Add the red chilli, mustard seeds and turmeric and cook for 1 minute, until fragrant. Be careful, as the mustard seeds can pop and spit when they get hot. Remove the pan from the heat to allow to cool slightly, then discard the chilli.

MAKE THE RAITA

400g thick Greek yoghurt

20g fresh dill, chopped (including the stems if they are tender)

1 tsp runny honey

¾ tsp fine sea salt

pinch of chilli flakes

Put the yoghurt, dill, honey and salt in a medium bowl and stir together, then use a spatula to scrape all the spiced oil and tempered spices from the pan into the yoghurt and stir again. Garnish with a pinch of chilli flakes on top.

This will keep in an airtight container or jar in the fridge for 1–2 days.

SERVES 4

— KHEERA PYAZ KA RAITA —
PICKLED CUCUMBER AND RED ONION RAITA

This classic raita has an unexpected sour tang from the pickled cucumber and red onion.

MAKE THE PICKLE

½ cucumber, peeled, deseeded and finely diced

½ small red onion, very finely diced

4 stems of fresh dill, roughly torn

2 tbsp white wine vinegar

1 tsp grated or finely chopped fresh ginger

½ tsp fine sea salt

Mix together the cucumber, red onion, dill, vinegar, ginger and salt in a small bowl and set aside for 30 minutes to lightly pickle, then drain.

MAKE THE RAITA

100g thick Greek yoghurt

30g shop-bought mayonnaise

¼ tsp fine sea salt

splash of good olive oil (extra virgin or regular)

Mix the yoghurt, mayonnaise and salt in a medium bowl, then drizzle in a few drops of good olive oil. Fold in the drained cucumber and red onion.
This will keep in an airtight container or jar in the fridge for 1–2 days.

SERVES 4

— ANAR KA RAITA —
AVOCADO, POMEGRANATE AND CORIANDER RAITA

Raita is usually served as a cooling element to a dish, but when I opened Pickle, I created this raita to make it more of a dish in its own right rather than an often-overlooked side. You could chop the avocados and fresh herbs by hand if blending it to a purée feels like too much trouble, but I prefer the flavours when they are all blended together.

> **PREP**
> Prep and measure out all the spices and ingredients before you start cooking so that everything is ready to go.

MAKE THE AVOCADO PURÉE

2 small ripe avocados, halved and stoned

25g fresh coriander

10g fresh mint leaves, plus extra to garnish

Scoop the avocados out of their skins and into a blender or food processor. Tear in the coriander, stalks and all, the mint leaves and **50ml water** and blend to a thick purée.

MAKE THE RAITA

450g thick Greek yoghurt

seeds of ½ pomegranate, plus extra to garnish

½ fresh green chilli, finely chopped

¼ tsp toasted cumin seeds, plus extra to garnish

¾ tsp fine sea salt

1 lemon wedge

Immediately transfer to a large bowl with the yoghurt and stir together before the avocado has a chance to oxidise and turn brown, then stir in the pomegranate seeds, green chilli, toasted cumin seeds, salt and a squeeze of lemon juice. Garnish with pomegranate and cumin seeds and a few small fresh mint leaves.

This is best eaten on the day it's made because it tends to turn a little grey when the avocado eventually does oxidise, but the flavour will still be good for up to 1–2 days if kept in an airtight container or jar in the fridge.

MAKES ABOUT **300G**

— AKHROT, NASHPATI KI CHUTNEY —
PEAR AND WALNUT CHUTNEY

Choose pears that are ripe but still quite firm, as you want them to hold their shape in this chutney. Serve this with the goats' cheese cakes on page 186 or as part of a cheeseboard.

> **PREP**
>
> Measure out your spices into two separate small bowls: one for the whole spices and one for the sugar, paprika, ground cinnamon and salt.
>
> Prep and measure out all the remaining ingredients before you start cooking so that everything is ready to go and the spices don't burn.

COOK THE WHOLE SPICES

20ml vegetable oil

3–4 green cardamom pods

1 small cinnamon stick

½ tsp cumin seeds

Heat the oil in a saucepan over a medium-high heat. Add the cardamom, cinnamon stick and cumin seeds and cook for 1 minute, until fragrant.

MAKE THE CHUTNEY

150ml distilled or white wine vinegar

100g caster sugar

1 tsp paprika

½ tsp ground cinnamon

1 tsp fine sea salt

2 firm pears, unpeeled, cored, halved and thinly sliced (300g)

Raise the heat to high, pour in the vinegar and let everything sizzle together for a minute. Stir in the sugar, paprika, ground cinnamon and salt. Cook for 1 minute, stirring, then add the pears.

Reduce the heat to medium-high and simmer for 20–30 minutes, stirring occasionally, until the pears are soft and translucent and the liquid has reduced quite a bit but taking care not to let it scorch on the bottom of the pan. Remove the pan from the heat and allow to cool.

 ## TOAST THE WALNUTS

50g walnut halves

While the chutney is cooking, toast the walnuts in a hot dry pan over a medium heat for a few minutes, stirring often, until golden. Tip out on to a plate and allow to cool.

 ## BRING IT ALL TOGETHER

Once the chutney has cooled, crush the walnuts a bit in your hands and crumble them in, stirring gently to combine.

This will keep in a sealed jar in the fridge for months.

SERVES 4

KHAJOOR, PALAK & HARA PYAZ KA RAITA
SPINACH, DATE AND SPRING ONION RAITA

Back when I was working there, the executive chef at the Oberoi Group in India was Rajiv Singh Gulshan, but everyone called him God or Lord Gulshan because of his vast knowledge and how highly esteemed he was by all who worked with him – and because he was the only chef in the entire group who refused to wear a chef's toque. He is the one who told me I should come to Dublin. He worked in Australia for a time but is back in India again, where he is now the dean of the Institute for Hotel Management in Gurgaon. I still have such high respect for him that if he were to call me tomorrow and tell me that he needed me, I would drop everything and go. I learned this recipe from him. I never would have thought to combine spinach, dates and spring onions in a raita, but its sweetness makes it a good accompaniment to anything spicy.

PREP
Prep and measure out all the spices and ingredients before you start cooking so that everything is ready to go.

BLANCH THE SPINACH

1 x 200g bag of baby spinach

Blanch the baby spinach in a small saucepan of boiling water just until it has wilted down, then drain and transfer to a bowl of iced water to stop it cooking any further and to keep its bright green colour. Let it sit for a few minutes, then drain and squeeze out as much water as possible before chopping.

MAKE THE RAITA

250g thick Greek yoghurt

4 Medjool dates, pitted and chopped

2 spring onions, white and green parts finely chopped

juice of ½ lemon

4–5 fresh mint leaves, shredded

½ tsp toasted cumin seeds

pinch of garam masala

½ tsp fine sea salt

pinch of freshly ground black pepper

Transfer the chopped spinach to a medium bowl with the rest of the ingredients and mix together. It's ready to eat now, but it will be even better if you can leave it for a little while to let the flavours marry together.

CHAPTER 8

✦

DESSERTS AND DRINKS

SERVES **6** TO **8**

— KHEER —
INDIAN RICE PUDDING

Whenever there is a celebration, festival or birthday in my family there will be rice pudding (kheer), so it always makes me think of the feasts we had at home. My sister and I would eat it very slowly to make it last until everyone else had finished their share. When I met my wife, Leena, this was the first thing she made for me.

PREP

Prep and measure out all the spices and ingredients before you start cooking so that everything is ready to go.

RINSE AND SOAK THE RICE

75g basmati rice

Rinse the rice a few times in a big bowl of water. After rinsing, leave the rice to soak for 30 minutes, then drain. Rinsing the rice like this gets rid of any impurities.

SOAK THE COCONUT

40g grated fresh coconut, desiccated coconut or dried coconut flakes

If you're using desiccated coconut or dried coconut flakes instead of fresh grated coconut, you need to soak it in a small bowl of hot water first.

MAKE THE RICE PUDDING

40g butter or ghee

4 green cardamom pods, lightly crushed open

50g sultanas

50g flaked almonds

20g chopped pistachios

2 litres full-fat milk

Melt the butter or ghee in a large heavy-based saucepan or casserole over a medium heat. Add the cardamom pods and drained rice and stir gently to coat the rice in the butter, then add the sultanas, almonds, pistachios and milk. Reduce the heat to low and simmer, uncovered, for about 40 minutes.

TO FINISH

90g caster sugar

80g almond or cashew butter

tiny pinch of saffron (10 threads)

few drops of rosewater (optional)

Add the sugar, nut butter, coconut (either the fresh grated coconut or the soaked and drained dried coconut), saffron and rosewater (if using). Simmer gently for another 10 minutes, stirring every now and then so that it doesn't stick to the bottom of the pan now that you've added the sugar. You want the rice to be completely soft and broken down in this pudding.

To serve This rice pudding can be served hot or cold, with a handful of chopped pistachios, cashews or walnuts and a few saffron threads scattered on top.

SERVES **6** TO **8**

— GHAI SAHIB KA SUJI HALWA —
GHAI SAHIB'S SEMOLINA PUDDING

My father was very fond of this pudding, which he would eat at any time of the day, not just as dessert. When I go home to India to visit, I stay up until 2am talking with my family and eventually someone will say that they're hungry again and we make this. The only argument then would be who would be the one to get up and go to the kitchen to make it.

> **PREP**
> Prep and measure out all the spices and ingredients before you start cooking so that everything is ready to go.

MAKE THE SUGAR SYRUP

360g caster sugar

Put the sugar and **450ml water** in a heavy-based saucepan over a medium-high heat, stirring occasionally until the sugar has dissolved. Remove the pan from the heat and set aside.

MAKE THE PUDDING

150g butter or ghee

4 green cardamom pods

200g semolina

50g raisins

40g flaked almonds

40g cashews

40g walnuts

Melt the butter or ghee with the cardamom pods in a large heavy-based saucepan over a medium-low heat, then add the semolina. Cook gently for 15–20 minutes, until the semolina starts to smell toasted and turns golden brown. Stir in the raisins and nuts and cook for 1 minute, then start to gradually add the sugar syrup, stirring continuously to avoid lumps forming. Keep stirring for a few more minutes. It will get thick, like the consistency of mashed potatoes, and will leave the sides and bottom of the pan.

To serve Spoon the warm semolina pudding into a serving dish and sprinkle a little orange zest over the top.

SERVES **4**

— GAJAR KA HALWA —
CARROT HALWA

The Gwalior state fair is one of the largest fairs in all of India. Haridwar Wala Restaurant is a pop-up that would come to the fair every year and was famous for its carrot halwa. The water content of Irish carrots is much higher than carrots grown in India, so the trick to this simple dessert is letting the milk completely evaporate, which takes about 45 minutes and a careful eye.

> **PREP**
> Prep and measure out all the spices and ingredients before you start cooking so that everything is ready to go.

60g butter or ghee

100g mix of golden sultanas, cashews and pistachios (nuts left whole)

2 green cardamom pods, crushed open

500g peeled and grated carrots (prepped weight)

60g caster sugar

500ml milk

Melt the butter or ghee in a large heavy-based saucepan over a gentle heat – it must be a low heat, otherwise the raisins will burn. Add the raisin and nut mix and the cardamom pods and cook for 1–2 minutes to plump up the raisins, then add the carrots.

Increase the heat to high and cook, stirring, for 2–3 minutes to cook off some of the water in the carrots. Add the sugar and continue to cook, still over a high heat and still stirring, for another 5 minutes, until the carrots are starting to caramelise and turn golden.

Pour in the milk, then reduce the heat to medium-low and simmer, stirring occasionally, until all the milk has completely evaporated – this should take about 30 minutes. At this point you'll see that the milk has turned into grainy granules, almost like granulated sugar. Keep cooking and stir almost constantly now for another 10–15 minutes, until it's very thick.

To serve *Serve hot with a spoonful of crème fraîche on top.*

SERVES **4**

— RASEDAR NASHPATI —
TURMERIC POACHED PEARS

This isn't a traditional dish, but I created it to offer a fruit dessert at Pickle that was familiar and simple but with spicing that was different to what people are used to with poached pears. If you need convincing with turmeric, this is the dish to convert you. The fresh turmeric adds a balancing bitter note to the sweet dish. Fresh turmeric works best here, as I find that using ground turmeric can make the syrup cloudy, but it will still be delicious if that's all you can find.

> **PREP**
> Prep and measure out all the spices and ingredients before you start cooking so that everything is ready to go.

POACH THE PEARS

- 250ml Chardonnay or Riesling wine
- juice of 1 large orange (keep the squeezed-out halves)
- 200g caster sugar
- 2–3 cloves
- 1 bay leaf
- 1 star anise
- 1 cinnamon stick
- 10g fresh turmeric, peeled and sliced, or 1 tsp ground turmeric
- 4 firm, ripe pears

Pour the wine and **750ml water** into a saucepan that the pears will fit into snugly. Pour in the orange juice, then add the orange halves to the pan too. Add the sugar, cloves, bay leaf, star anise, cinnamon stick and turmeric and bring to the boil, stirring to dissolve the sugar.

Peel the pears and remove the hard core from the base, then gently add them to the poaching liquid and reduce the heat to low. Press a sheet of baking paper directly on top of the pears to keep them submerged. Simmer for anywhere from 25 to 45 minutes – it all depends on the ripeness of the pears you're using. The pears should be so soft that a small sharp knife can be inserted with no resistance, but take care not to overcook them or they'll get too mushy.

MAKE THE SYRUP

Use a slotted spoon to remove the pears from the pan and set aside. Bring the poaching liquid back to the boil and keep boiling until it has reduced to a thick syrup – this may take quite some time to get it to the right consistency. Pour through a fine-mesh sieve to strain out the orange halves and spices.

To serve Serve one pear per person with star anise ice cream (page 256) or shop-bought vanilla ice cream, softly whipped cream or crème fraîche and some of the syrup spooned over.

SERVES **4**

— KESARI ANANAS —
TANDOORI-STYLE PINEAPPLE

I was inspired to make this dish by the pineapple chop in *The French Laundry Cookbook*. The chilli in the coconut, basil and chilli ice cream cuts through the sweetness.

> **PREP**
> Prep and measure out all the spices and ingredients before you start cooking so that everything is ready to go.

PREPARE THE PINEAPPLE

1 large ripe pineapple

Cut off the top and bottom of the pineapple, then slice away all the tough skin and trim off all the brown 'eyes'. Cut the pineapple into quarters and slice away the tough inner core, then cut each quarter in half so that you have eight large pieces.

POACH THE PINEAPPLE

200g caster sugar
3–4 star anise
1 cinnamon stick
large pinch of saffron

Put the pineapple, sugar, star anise, cinnamon stick, saffron and **200ml water** into a saucepan. Cover and bring to the boil, then reduce the heat to very low and simmer gently for 25–30 minutes, until the sugar syrup has thickened, the pineapple has become a beautiful golden colour from the saffron and a knife goes through it easily.

MAKE THE SYRUP

Using a slotted spoon, transfer the pineapple to a bowl. Put the pan back over a high heat and boil to reduce the poaching liquid to a thick syrup, but take care that you don't let it reduce too much or it will scorch and burn; keep in mind that it will thicken more as it cools. Remove the whole spices from the syrup at this point.

ROAST THE PINEAPPLE

50g caster sugar
4 green cardamom pods, ground in a pestle and mortar (½ tsp ground)

Preheat the grill and line a baking tray with foil.

Put the sugar and ground cardamom in a wide, shallow bowl and stir to combine. Remove the pineapple from the bowl, shaking gently to remove any excess poaching liquid, then toss in the spiced sugar until evenly coated all over and place on the lined baking tray.

Roast the pineapple pieces under the grill until they are nicely charred and caramelised, but keep a close eye on them so that the sugar doesn't go too far and burn. (Alternatively, you could finish this on the barbecue.)

To serve *Serve warm with a scoop of coconut, basil and chilli ice cream (page 254) or shop-bought vanilla ice cream and spoon over the reduced syrup.*

DESSERTS AND DRINKS

MAKES ABOUT 18

— KHAJA —
DATE AND COCONUT FILO PASTRIES

I have seen this crisp baked pastry, which is sometimes sweetened or sometimes quite plain, sold in huge quantities during Muslim religious festivals in India. I've used a date mixture to fill this pastry and I serve it with an orange and lime syrup for a delicious dessert. If you have some filling left over, try stirring it into porridge as a breakfast treat.

PREP
Prep and measure out all the spices and ingredients before you start cooking so that everything is ready to go.

MAKE THE FILLING

60g salted butter

500g dates, pitted and finely chopped

150g desiccated coconut

80g mixed nuts (almonds, walnuts, pistachios), finely chopped

80g candied orange peel

160ml orange juice

1½ tsp toasted fennel seeds, crushed

Melt the butter in a saucepan over a low heat, then stir in the dates, coconut, nuts, orange peel, orange juice and fennel seeds and cook until the dates have softened a little.

ASSEMBLE THE PASTRIES

2 x 270g packs of filo pastry, thawed

180g butter or ghee, melted

Brush one sheet of filo pastry with some of the melted butter or ghee, place a second sheet directly on top and brush that with melted butter or ghee too, then cut lengthways into three long rectangles.

Put 1 heaped tablespoon of the filling in the corner of the short edge of the rectangle closest to you. Take that corner of the pastry and fold it diagonally and up to the opposite side of the rectangle to form a triangle, then fold that triangle up and over itself to form another triangle. Repeat all the way up the rectangle until there is only one triangle (or portion of a triangle) left to fold, then fold one last time to seal. Set aside on a baking tray lined with non-stick baking paper and repeat with the rest of the pastry sheets and filling. Chill in the fridge for 20 minutes.

BAKE THE PASTRIES

Preheat the oven to 210°C/190°C fan/gas 6.

Brush the tops of the pastries with a little more melted butter, then bake in the preheated oven for about 20 minutes, until golden brown and crisp. Set aside to cool slightly.

MAKE THE ORANGE AND LIME SYRUP

180g caster sugar

300ml orange juice

juice of 1 lime

While the pastries are baking, put the caster sugar, orange juice and lime juice in a small saucepan. Bring to the boil, then lower the heat and simmer until it has reduced to a thick syrup. Set aside.

FINISH WITH THE CARDAMOM SUGAR

2 tbsp caster sugar

4 green cardamom pods, ground in a pestle and mortar (½ tsp ground)

Mix together the caster sugar and ground cardamom in a small bowl, then sprinkle this over the cooled pastries.

To serve *Place the filo pastries on cold plates, spoon over the orange and lime syrup and serve with softly whipped cream.*

SERVES **4**

— KULFI —
SAFFRON AND CARDAMOM ICE CREAM

Kulfi is an eggless ice cream eaten only in the summertime – a man with a pushcart goes around selling kulfi on sticks, a bit like the Mr Whippy van here! Mango or pistachio work well for kulfi, or even dried fig, which has become popular in India. Time is the most important ingredient in homemade kulfi, as you're reducing 2 litres of milk to 750ml. You'll find liquid glucose in the baking section of your supermarket – it's widely available.

> **PREP**
> Prep and measure out all the spices and ingredients before you start cooking so that everything is ready to go.

MAKE THE KULFI

6–8 green cardamom pods

2 litres full-fat milk

2 big pinches of saffron (0.5g if your scale can measure such a small amount)

3 tbsp liquid glucose

150g caster sugar

50g chopped pistachios, plus extra to serve

300ml double cream

few drops of rosewater (optional)

Crush the cardamom pods with a rolling pin to release the seeds, then put them in a large heavy-based saucepan or a large stock pot with the milk and bring to the boil, keeping a careful eye on it so that it doesn't boil over. Reduce the heat to medium-high, add the saffron and simmer, stirring occasionally, until it has reduced right down to 750ml and is nice and thick. This will easily take at least 1–1½ hours, so put the pan on the back burner while you get on with other things.

Once the milk has reduced, whisk in the liquid glucose, then pour it into a large jug or bowl through a fine-mesh sieve to strain out the cardamom pods and any milk solids. Add the sugar, stirring until it has dissolved in the hot milk, then add the nuts, cream and rosewater (if using). Allow to cool.

FREEZE

Freeze in an ice cream machine according to the manufacturer's instructions. If you don't have a machine but you have a food processor, pour the mixture into a large freezerproof ziplock bag and freeze it into a flat sheet. Once it's frozen solid, break it up into large pieces and pulse in your food processor until smooth, then freeze again in an airtight container.

To serve Serve two or three small scoops per person with a drizzle of shop-bought raspberry coulis, a pinch of desiccated coconut and some extra chopped pistachios scattered on top.

Serves **4** to **6**

— KHOPRA TULSI ICE CREAM —
COCONUT, BASIL AND CHILLI ICE CREAM

I created this ice cream specifically to go with the tandoori-style pineapple on page 248. It may sound like an unusual combination at first, but it all works together beautifully.

INFUSE THE MILK AND COCONUT CREAM

2 x 160ml tins of coconut cream

250ml full-fat milk

2 fresh basil sprigs, chopped

Put the coconut cream, milk and fresh basil in a large saucepan and bring to the boil – the coconut cream will melt in, so you don't need to try to whisk it beforehand. Immediately remove the pan from the heat and set aside for 2 hours to let the basil infuse the coconut cream and milk.

PREPARE THE CHILLI

1 fresh red chilli, deseeded and finely chopped

juice of ½ lime

1 tbsp honey

Put the finely chopped red chilli, lime juice and honey in a small bowl and microwave for 20 seconds just to warm everything together. Set aside for 20–30 minutes to let the flavours marry together.

MAKE THE ICE CREAM

100g caster sugar

3 egg yolks (you want 60g of yolks)

20g desiccated coconut, toasted

Whisk the sugar and egg yolks together in a large bowl, then slowly whisk in the infused coconut cream and milk.

Pour the mixture into a clean saucepan and put it over a medium heat, stirring continuously until the mixture thickens and coats the back of the spoon. Make sure the mixture doesn't boil.

Pour through a fine-mesh sieve, then allow to cool before stirring in the chilli mixture and the toasted coconut.

Churn the mixture in an ice cream machine according to the manufacturer's instructions. If you don't have an ice cream machine but you do have a food processor, pour the base mixture into a large freezerproof ziplock bag and freeze it into a flat sheet. Once it's frozen solid, break it up into large pieces and pulse in your food processor until smooth, then freeze again in a regular airtight container.

SERVES **6** TO **8**

— CHAKRI PHOOL ICE CREAM —
STAR ANISE ICE CREAM

This is the perfect complement to the turmeric poached pears on page 246, but it would be just as good on its own. I've used star anise to infuse the cream and milk, but the base recipe is very basic so you can experiment with it as you like. Try using cinnamon sticks instead of the star anise or for a more unusual but equally delicious ice cream, try fennel seeds and a splash of sambuca or a good pinch of garam masala. You could even stir in some mango purée.

INFUSE THE CREAM AND MILK

500ml cream

500ml milk

8 star anise

½ vanilla pod, split in half lengthways and seeds scraped out

Put the cream, milk, star anise and the vanilla seeds and pod in a large saucepan and bring to the boil, then immediately remove the pan from the heat and set aside for 3 hours to let the star anise infuse the cream and milk. Remove the star anise and vanilla pod after this time and discard them.

MAKE THE ICE CREAM

200g caster sugar

8–9 large egg yolks (you need 160g egg yolks)

Whisk the sugar and egg yolks together in a large bowl, then slowly whisk in the infused cream and milk.

Pour the mixture back into a clean saucepan and put it over a medium heat, stirring continuously until the mixture thickens and coats the back of the spoon. Make sure the mixture doesn't boil.

Pour through a fine-mesh sieve, then allow to cool.

Churn the mixture in an ice cream machine according to the manufacturer's instructions. If you don't have an ice cream machine but you do have a food processor, pour the base mixture into a large freezerproof ziplock bag and freeze it into a flat sheet. Once it's frozen solid, break it up into large pieces and pulse in your food processor until smooth, then freeze again in a regular airtight container.

SERVES 4

— AAM KI LASSI —
MANGO LASSI

In India, mango is the king of fruits. The saffron is optional but it gives the lassi a gorgeous golden colour. The glasses in India that we drink lassi out of are made of brass, have a capacity of around 800ml and can weigh up to 1 kilogram just on their own – without the drink even added in.

MAKE THE MANGO PURÉE

500g peeled and diced ripe mango

Blend the mango to a smooth purée in a NutriBullet or blender – you should have about 400ml.

MAKE THE LASSI

400g thick Greek yoghurt

60g caster sugar

2 green cardamom pods, ground in a pestle and mortar (a pinch of ground powder)

Whisk together the mango purée, yoghurt and **100ml water** in a large bowl, then whisk in the sugar and ground cardamom. It's best to let the lassi sit for a little while to allow the sugar to dissolve, but it's also delicious to drink straightaway.

To serve Serve in small glasses with a pinch of saffron on top (optional).

MAKES **700ML**

— CHAAS —
SALTY SPICED LASSI

A salty lassi might sound strange at first if you've only ever had the sweet kind, but it is a refreshing, cooling drink on a scorching hot summer day in southern India.

PREP

Measure out your spices into two separate small bowls: one for the whole spices and the pinch of turmeric and one for the salt, cumin and pepper.

Prep and measure out all the remaining ingredients before you start cooking so that everything is ready to go.

CRUSH THE HERBS AND SPICES

1 tbsp chopped fresh mint, plus extra to garnish

1 tbsp chopped fresh coriander

1½ tsp grated or finely chopped fresh ginger

¼ tsp finely chopped fresh green chilli

Crush the fresh herbs, ginger and green chilli together in a pestle and mortar.

COOK THE WHOLE SPICES

2 tsp oil

1 dried red chilli, seeds removed

½ tsp mustard seeds

pinch of ground turmeric

Heat the oil in a small frying pan over a medium heat. Add the dried red chilli, mustard seeds and turmeric and cook for 1 minute, until fragrant. Remove the pan from the heat.

MAKE THE LASSI

400g thick Greek yoghurt

1 tsp fine sea salt

¼ tsp ground cumin

¼ tsp freshly ground black pepper

Whisk together the yoghurt, salt, cumin, black pepper and **300ml water** in a large bowl or jug, then pour in the crushed herbs and the spiced oil and whisk again. Unlike sweet lassis, this one is meant to be quite thin.

To serve *It's best to let the lassi sit for a little while to allow the salt to dissolve, but it's also delicious to drink straightaway over ice. Garnish with a few small fresh mint leaves.*

INDEX

A

almonds:
Ghai Sahib's Semolina Pudding/*Ghai Sahib Ka Suji Halwa*, 242–3
Indian Rice Pudding/*Kheer*, 240–41
Lamb Shanks with Tomatoes, Almonds and Yoghurt/*Nalli Ki Kaliya*, 84–5
Wild Mushrooms and Sweetcorn with Almonds/*Makai Khumbh Badam Ki Subzi*, 190–91
apple: Apple and Fennel Salad/*Saunf Sev Ka Salaad*, 199
Mint and Coriander Chutney/*Dhaniya Pudina Ki Chutney*, 224–5
apricots: Chicken Curry with Dried Apricots/*Murgh Khubani*, 48–9
asparagus: Asparagus with Coconut and Mustard Seeds/*Asparagus Poriyal*, 196–7
Sunil's Stir-Fried Vegetables/*Subz Miloni*, 178–9
aubergines:
Bengali Babu's Aubergine and Potato Curry/*Aloo Baingan Ka Salan*, 138–9
Home-Style Fish Curry with Vegetables/*Meen Curry*, 120–21
Punjabi Aubergine Mash/*Baingan Bharta*, 194–5
Sweet-and-Sour Aubergine Chutney/*Baingan Chutney*, 225–6
avocado:
Avocado, Pomegranate and Coriander Raita/*Anar Ka Raita*, 232–3
Jumbo Prawns with Mango and Avocado Salad/*Tandoori Jhinga*, 98–9

B

Baby Spinach with Garlic and Fennel/*Chonka Lahsooni Patta*, 182
beans:
Hyderabadi Vegetable Korma/*Hyderabadi Subz Qurma*, 132–3
Leena's Kidney Bean Curry/*Rajmah Chawal*, 140–41
Potatoes and Fine Beans/*Aloo Phali*, 180–81
Sunil's Stir-Fried Vegetables/*Subz Miloni*, 178–9
Bengali Babu's Aubergine and Potato Curry/*Aloo Baingan Ka Salan*, 138–9
Biryani, Chicken/*Murgh Biryani*, 38–41
Black Pepper Chicken Curry/*Murgh Kali Mirch*, 28–9
Bombay Potatoes/*Mumbai Aloo Masala*, 168–9
Braised Lamb with Whole Spices/*Lucknowi Raan*, 86–9
bread:
Chilli and Cumin Naan, 210–13
Garlic and Coriander Naan, 210–13
Khasta Roti, 214–15
Plain Naan, 210–13
Poori, 205
Potato Flatbreads/*Aloo Paratha*, 216–17
Sunil's Garlic Bread, 218–19
broccoli:
Broccoli and Peppers with Pumpkin Seeds/*Hari Gobi Shimla Mirch*, 198
Sunil's Stir-Fried Vegetables/*Subz Miloni*, 178–9
Butter Chicken, Easy/*Punjabi Murgh Makhani*, 30–33
butternut squash, *see* pumpkin

C

Cardamom and Saffron Chicken Kebabs/*Murgh Malai Kebabs*, 26–7
carrots:
Carrot Halwa/*Gajar Ka Halwa*, 244–5
Home-Style Fish Curry with Vegetables/*Meen Curry*, 120–21
Hyderabadi Vegetable Korma/*Hyderabadi Subz Qurma*, 132–3
Vegetable Roll/*Kolkata Kathi Kebab*, 150–51
cashews:
Carrot Halwa/*Gajar Ka Halwa*, 244–5
Chicken Korma/*Murgh Qorma*, 34–5
Ghai Sahib's Semolina Pudding/*Ghai Sahib Ka Suji Halwa*, 242–3
Tomato and Cashew Chutney/*Bengali Chutney*, 222–3
cauliflower:
Cauliflower with Turmeric and Ginger/*Adraki Gobhi*, 184–5
Hyderabadi Vegetable Korma/*Hyderabadi Subz Qurma*, 132–3
Spiced Whole Roasted Cauliflower/*Gobhi Musallam*, 162–3
cheese:
Goats' Cheese Cakes/*Goats' Cheese Tikki*, 186–9
Paneer and Pea Curry/*Matar Paneer*, 152–3
Paneer Cheese Skewers/*Paneer Tikka*, 154–7
Saag Paneer/*Palak Paneer*, 148–9
Chettinad, Chicken/*Murgh Chettiar*, 36–7
chicken:
Black Pepper Chicken Curry/*Murgh Kali Mirch*, 28–9
Cardamom and Saffron Chicken Kebabs/*Murgh Malai Kebabs*, 26–7

Chicken Biryani/*Murgh Biryani*, 38–41
Chicken Chettinad (a real Madras)/*Murgh Chettiar*, 36–7
Chicken Curry with Dried Apricots/*Murgh Khubani*, 48–9
Chicken Curry with Spinach, Herbs and Cream/*Palak Murgh*, 50–51
Chicken Jalfrezi/*Murgh Jalfrezi*, 46–7
Chicken Korma/*Murgh Qorma*, 34–5
Easy Butter Chicken/*Punjabi Murgh Makhani*, 30–33
Home-Style Chicken Curry/*Murgh Rasedar*, 22–3
Lucknowi Chicken Curry/*Murgh Mughlai*, 24
Oven-Roasted Chicken Wings/*Fauzi Kadak Pankhuri*, 25
Tandoori-Style Chicken/*Tandoori Murgh*, 42–5
chickpeas:
Chickpea Curry with Poori/*Chana Bhatura*, 136–7
Sweet Potato and Chickpea Curry with Rack of Lamb/*Bengali Babu's Chana Gosht*, 76–7
Warm Chickpea, Mango and Coconut Salad/*Sundal*, 166–7
chillies, 18
Chilli and Cumin Naan, 210–13
Coconut, Basil and Chilli Ice Cream/*Khopra Tulsi Ice Cream*, 254–5
chutneys:
Mint and Coriander Chutney/*Dhaniya Pudina Ki Chutney*, 224–5
Pear and Walnut Chutney/*Akhrot, Nashpati Ki Chutney*, 234–5
Sweet-and-Sour Aubergine Chutney/*Baingan Chutney*, 225–6
Tomato and Cashew Chutney/*Bengali Chutney*, 222–3
clams: Goan-Style Mixed Seafood Curry/*Samundari Khazana*, 100–103
coconut:
Asparagus with Coconut and Mustard Seeds/*Asparagus Poriyal*, 196–7
Chicken Chettinad (a real Madras)/*Murgh Chettiar*, 36–7
Coconut Fish Curry/*Meen Moilee*, 104–5
Coconut, Basil and Chilli Ice Cream/*Khopra Tulsi Ice Cream*, 254–5
Date and Coconut Filo Pastries/*Khaja*, 250–51
Pork Belly Ribs with Coconut, Mango and Star Anise/*Achari Pasliyan*, 54–7
Warm Chickpea, Mango and Coconut Salad/*Sundal*, 166–7
cockles: Goan-Style Mixed Seafood Curry/*Samundari Khazana*, 100–103
cod: Punjabi Fish Fingers/*Machhi Pakora*, 115
coriander (fresh):
Avocado, Pomegranate and Coriander Raita/*Anar Ka Raita*, 232–3
Creamy Lamb Korma with Fresh Coriander/*Dhaniwal Qorma*, 74–5

Garlic and Coriander Naan, 210–13
Mint and Coriander Chutney/*Dhaniya Pudina Ki Chutney*, 224–5
Potatoes with Cumin and Fresh Coriander/*Jeera Aloo*, 183
Saag Paneer/*Palak Paneer*, 148–9
courgettes:
Home-Style Fish Curry with Vegetables/*Meen Curry*, 120–21
Prawn and Courgette Curry/*Lau Chingri*, 114
Sunil's Stir-Fried Vegetables/*Subz Miloni*, 178–9
Vegetable Roll/*Kolkata Kathi Kebab*, 150–51
crab: Goan-Style Mixed Seafood Curry/*Samundari Khazana*, 100–103
Creamy Lamb Korma with Fresh Coriander/*Dhaniwal Qorma*, 74–5
Crispy Prawns with Dill Raita/*Karwari Jhinga*, 96–7
cucumber: Pickled Cucumber and Red Onion Raita/*Kheera Pyaz Ka Raita*, 230–31
Curried Prawns/*Bhopali Jhinga*, 112–13

D

dal:
Home-Style Red Lentil Dal/*Malka Masoor Dal*, 128–9
Rustic Yellow Split Pea Dal/*Tadka Dal*, 130–31
dates:
Date and Coconut Filo Pastries/*Khaja*, 250–51
Spinach, Date and Spring Onion Raita/*Khajoor, Palak & Hara Pyaz Ka Raita*, 236–7
Dill Raita/*Soya Patta Raita*, 228–9

E

Easy Butter Chicken/*Punjabi Murgh Makhani*, 30–33
eggs:
Egg Curry/*Anda Curry*, 144–6
Indian Scrambled Eggs/*Akuri*, 142–3
Indian-Spiced Scotch Eggs/*Nargisi Kofta*, 58–61

F

fennel: Apple and Fennel Salad/*Saunf Sev Ka Salaad*, 199
fish:
Coconut Fish Curry/*Meen Moilee*, 104–5
Fish Cakes with Masala Mayo/*Machhi Ki Tikki*, 106–9
Home-Style Fish Curry with Vegetables/*Meen Curry*, 120–21

Oven-Roasted Sea Bass/*Tandoori Machi*, 116–17
Pan-Fried Mackerel/*Tawa Fish Fry*, 122–3
Punjabi Fish Fingers/*Machhi Pakora*, 115
Salmon with Yoghurt, Mustard and Turmeric/*Doi Maach*, 118–19
see also shellfish

G

garlic, 16
  Baby Spinach with Garlic and Fennel/*Chonka Lahsooni Patta*, 182
  Garlic and Coriander Naan, 210–13
  Sunil's Garlic Bread, 218–19
Ghai Sahib's Semolina Pudding/*Ghai Sahib Ka Suji Halwa*, 242–3
Goan Meatball Curry/*Keema Kofta Curry*, 68–71
Goan-Style Mixed Seafood Curry/*Samundari Khazana*, 100–103
goat:
Goat on Toast/*Keema Pao*, 90–93
  Goat Shanks with Tomatoes, Almonds and Yoghurt/*Nalli Ki Kaliya*, 84–5
Goats' Cheese Cakes/*Goats' Cheese Tikki*, 186–9

H

hake: Punjabi Fish Fingers/*Machhi Pakora*, 115
halibut: Home-Style Fish Curry with Vegetables/*Meen Curry*, 120–21
Halwa, Carrot/*Gajar Ka Halwa*, 244–5
herbs, fresh, 16
  Chicken Curry with Spinach, Herbs and Cream/*Palak Murgh*, 50–51
  Potatoes with Fresh Herbs and Pomegranate/*Aloo Chaat*, 170–71
Home-Style Chicken Curry/*Murgh Rasedar*, 22–3
Home-Style Fish Curry with Vegetables/*Meen Curry*, 120–21
Home-Style Red Lentil Dal/*Malka Masoor Dal*, 128–9
Hyderabadi Vegetable Korma/*Hyderabadi Subz Qurma*, 132–3

I

ice cream:
Coconut, Basil and Chilli Ice Cream/*Khopra Tulsi Ice Cream*, 254–5
  Saffron and Cardamom Ice Cream/*Kulfi*, 252–3
  Star Anise Ice Cream/*Chakri Phool Ice Cream*, 256–7
Indian Lamb Patties/*Shami Kebab*, 62–5
Indian Rice Pudding/*Kheer*, 240–41
Indian Scrambled Eggs/*Akuri*, 142–3
Indian-Spiced Scotch Eggs/*Nargisi Kofta*, 58–61

J

Jalfrezi, Chicken/*Murgh Jalfrezi*, 46–7
Jumbo Prawns with Mango and Avocado Salad/*Tandoori Jhinga*, 98–9

K

kebabs:
Cardamom and Saffron Chicken Kebabs/*Murgh Malai Kebabs*, 26–7
  Paneer Cheese Skewers/*Paneer Tikka*, 154–7
kewra water, 24
Khasta Roti, 214–15
korma, 34
  Chicken Korma/*Murgh Qorma*, 34–5
  Creamy Lamb Korma with Fresh Coriander/*Dhaniwal Qorma*, 74–5
  Hyderabadi Vegetable Korma/*Hyderabadi Subz Qurma*, 132–3

L

lamb:
Braised Lamb with Whole Spices/*Lucknowi Raan*, 86–9
  Creamy Lamb Korma with Fresh Coriander/*Dhaniwal Qorma*, 74–5
  Goan Meatball Curry/*Keema Kofta Curry*, 68–71
  Indian Lamb Patties/*Shami Kebab*, 62–5
  Indian-Spiced Scotch Eggs/*Nargisi Kofta*, 58–61
  Lamb Curry with Himalayan Spices/*Chha Gosht*, 82–3
  Lamb Mince and Pea Curry/*Keema Matar*, 72–3
  Lamb Samosas, 172–7
  Lamb Shanks with Tomatoes, Almonds and Yoghurt/*Nalli Ki Kaliya*, 84–5
  Railway Lamb Curry/*Aloo Gosht*, 78–81
  Sweet Potato and Chickpea Curry with Rack of Lamb/*Bengali Babu's Chana Gosht*, 76–7
  Tandoori Lamb Chops/*Gosht Ki Champain*, 66–7
lassi:
Mango Lassi/*Aam Ki Lassi*, 258–9
  Salty Spiced Lassi/*Chaas*, 260–61
Leena's Kidney Bean Curry/*Rajmah Chawal*, 140–41
Lemon Rice/*Nimbu Wale Chawal*, 206–7
lentils:
Home-Style Red Lentil Dal/*Malka Masoor Dal*, 128–9
  Mulligatawny Soup/*Dal Shorba*, 126–7
Lucknowi Chicken Curry/*Murgh Mughlai*, 24

M

Mackerel, Pan-Fried/*Tawa Fish Fry*, 122-3
Madras: Chicken Chettinad/*Murgh Chettiar*, 36-7
mangetout: Sunil's Stir-Fried Vegetables/*Subz Miloni*, 178-9
mango:
    Jumbo Prawns with Mango and Avocado Salad/*Tandoori Jhinga*, 98-9
    Mango Lassi/*Aam Ki Lassi*, 258-9
    Pork Belly Ribs with Coconut, Mango and Star Anise/*Achari Pasliyan*, 54-7
    Warm Chickpea, Mango and Coconut Salad/*Sundal*, 166-7
mayonnaise: Masala Mayo, 107
mint:
    Mint and Coriander Chutney/*Dhaniya Pudina Ki Chutney*, 224-5
    Salty Spiced Lassi/*Chaas*, 260-61
Mulligatawny Soup/*Dal Shorba*, 126-7
mushrooms:
    Hyderabadi Vegetable Korma/*Hyderabadi Subz Qurma*, 132-3
    Sunil's Stir-Fried Vegetables/*Subz Miloni*, 178-9
    Wild Mushrooms and Sweetcorn with Almonds/*Makai Khumbh Badam Ki Subzi*, 190-91
mussels: Goan-Style Mixed Seafood Curry/*Samundari Khazana*, 100-103

N

naan, 210-13
    Chilli and Cumin, 212
    Garlic and Coriander, 212
    Plain, 212

O

onions:
Pickled Cucumber and Red Onion Raita/*Kheera Pyaz Ka Raita*, 230-31
    Pickled Red Onions/*Sirka Pyaz*, 200-201
    Spiced Basmati Rice with Peas and Red Onion/*Pulao*, 208-9
    Spinach, Date and Spring Onion Raita/*Khajoor, Palak & Hara Pyaz Ka Raita*, 236-7
Oven-Roasted Chicken Wings/*Fauzi Kadak Pankhuri*, 25
Oven-Roasted Sea Bass/*Tandoori Machi*, 116-17

P

Pan-Fried Mackerel/*Tawa Fish Fry*, 122-3
paneer:
    Paneer and Pea Curry/*Matar Paneer*, 152-3
    Paneer Cheese Skewers/*Paneer Tikka*, 154-7
    Saag Paneer/*Palak Paneer*, 148-9
Pastries, Date and Coconut Filo/*Khaja*, 250-51
patties/cakes:
    Fish Cakes with Masala Mayo/*Machhi Ki Tikki*, 106-9
    Goats' Cheese Cakes/*Goats' Cheese Tikki*, 186-9
    Indian Lamb Patties/*Shami Kebab*, 62-5
    Stuffed Potato Cakes/*Aloo Tikki*, 158-61
pears:
    Pear and Walnut Chutney/*Akhrot, Nashpati Ki Chutney*, 234-5
    Turmeric Poached Pears/*Rasedar Nashpati*, 246-7
peas:
    Hyderabadi Vegetable Korma/*Hyderabadi Subz Qurma*, 132-3
    Lamb Mince and Pea Curry/*Keema Matar*, 72-3
    Paneer and Pea Curry/*Matar Paneer*, 152-3
    Spiced Basmati Rice with Peas and Red Onion/*Pulao*, 208-9
    Stuffed Potato Cakes/*Aloo Tikki*, 158-61
    see also split peas
peppers:
Broccoli and Peppers with Pumpkin Seeds/*Hari Gobi Shimla Mirch*, 198
    Paneer Cheese Skewer/*Paneer Tikka*, 154-7
    Vegetable Roll/*Kolkata Kathi Kebab*, 150-51
Pickled Cucumber and Red Onion Raita/*Kheera Pyaz Ka Raita*, 230-31
Pickled Red Onions/*Sirka Pyaz*, 200-201
pineapple:
Mulligatawny Soup/*Dal Shorba*, 126-7
    Tandoori-Style Pineapple/*Kesari Ananas*, 248-9
pistachios:
Carrot Halwa/*Gajar Ka Halwa*, 244-5
    Indian Rice Pudding/*Kheer*, 240-41
Plain Boiled Basmati Rice/*Safed Chawal*, 204
Plain Naan, 210-13
pomegranate:
Avocado, Pomegranate and Coriander Raita/*Anar Ka Raita*, 232-3
    Potatoes with Fresh Herbs and Pomegranate/*Aloo Chaat*, 170-71
Poori, 205
    Chickpea Curry with Poori/*Chana Bhatura*, 136-7
    Potato Curry with Poori/*Poori Bhaji*, 134-5
Pork Belly Ribs with Coconut, Mango and Star Anise/*Achari Pasliyan*, 54-7

potatoes:
Bengali Babu's Aubergine and Potato Curry/*Aloo Baingan Ka Salan*, 138–9
   Bombay Potatoes/*Mumbai Aloo Masala*, 168–9
   Fish Cakes with Masala Mayo/*Machhi Ki Tikki*, 106–9
   Home-Style Fish Curry with Vegetables/*Meen Curry*, 120–21
   Potato Curry with Poori/*Poori Bhaji*, 134–5
   Potato Flatbreads/*Aloo Paratha*, 216–17
   Potato Samosas, 172–7
   Potatoes and Fine Beans/*Aloo Phali*, 180–81
   Potatoes with Cumin and Fresh Coriander/*Jeera Aloo*, 183
   Potatoes with Fresh Herbs and Pomegranate/*Aloo Chaat*, 170–71
   Railway Lamb Curry/*Aloo Gosht*, 78–81
   Stuffed Potato Cakes/*Aloo Tikki*, 158–61
prawns:
Crispy Prawns with Dill Raita/*Karwari Jhinga*, 96–7
   Curried Prawns/*Bhopali Jhinga*, 112–13
   Goan-Style Mixed Seafood Curry/*Samundari Khazana*, 100–103
   Jumbo Prawns with Mango and Avocado Salad/*Tandoori Jhinga*, 98–9
   Prawn and Courgette Curry/*Lau Chingri*, 114
   Spicy Prawn Curry/*Tawa Jhinga Masala*, 110–11
puddings:
Ghai Sahib's Semolina Pudding/*Ghai Sahib Ka Suji Halwa*, 242–3
Indian Rice Pudding/*Kheer*, 240–41
pumpkin: Sweet-and-Sour Pumpkin/*Khatta Meetha Kaddu*, 192–3
pumpkin seeds: Broccoli and Peppers with Pumpkin Seeds/*Hari Gobi Shimla Mirch*, 198
Punjabi Aubergine Mash/*Baingan Bharta*, 194–5
Punjabi Fish Fingers/*Machhi Pakora*, 115

R

Railway Lamb Curry/*Aloo Gosht*, 78–81
raita:
Avocado, Pomegranate and Coriander Raita/*Anar Ka Raita*, 232–3
   Crispy Prawns with Dill Raita/*Karwari Jhinga*, 96–7
   Dill Raita/*Soya Patta Raita*, 228–9
   Pickled Cucumber and Red Onion Raita/*Kheera Pyaz Ka Raita*, 230–31
   Spinach, Date and Spring Onion Raita/*Khajoor, Palak & Hara Pyaz Ka Raita*, 236–7
rice:
Chicken Biryani/*Murgh Biryani*, 38–41
Indian Rice Pudding/*Kheer*, 240–41
Lemon Rice/*Nimbu Wale Chawal*, 206–7
Plain Boiled Basmati Rice/*Safed Chawal*, 204
Spiced Basmati Rice with Peas and Red Onion/*Pulao*, 208–9
Roti, 214–15
Rustic Yellow Split Pea Dal/*Tadka Dal*, 130–31

S

Saag Paneer/*Palak Paneer*, 148–9
Saffron and Cardamom Ice Cream/*Kulfi*, 252–3
salads:
Apple and Fennel Salad/*Saunf Sev Ka Salaad*, 199
   Jumbo Prawns with Mango and Avocado Salad/*Tandoori Jhinga*, 98–9
   Warm Chickpea, Mango and Coconut Salad/*Sundal*, 166–7
Salmon with Yoghurt, Mustard and Turmeric/*Doi Maach*, 118–19
Salty Spiced Lassi/*Chaas*, 260–61
samosas, 172–7
   lamb, 172–7
   potato, 172–7
   spinach and sultana, 172–7
sea bass/bream:
Coconut Fish Curry/*Meen Moilee*, 104–5
   Oven-Roasted Sea Bass/*Tandoori Machi*, 116–17
Semolina Pudding, Ghai Sahib's/*Ghai Sahib Ka Suji Halwa*, 242–3
shellfish:
Crispy Prawns with Dill Raita/*Karwari Jhinga*, 96–7
   Curried Prawns/*Bhopali Jhinga*, 112–13
   Goan-Style Mixed Seafood Curry/*Samundari Khazana*, 100–103
   Jumbo Prawns with Mango and Avocado Salad/*Tandoori Jhinga*, 98–9
   Prawn and Courgette Curry/*Lau Chingri*, 114
   Spicy Prawn Curry/*Tawa Jhinga Masala*, 110–11
Soup, Mulligatawny/*Dal Shorba*, 126–7
Spiced Basmati Rice with Peas and Red Onion/*Pulao*, 208–9
Spiced Whole Roasted Cauliflower/*Gobhi Musallam*, 162–3
spices, 16–18
Spicy Prawn Curry/*Tawa Jhinga Masala*, 110–11
spinach:
Baby Spinach with Garlic and Fennel/*Chonka Lahsooni Patta*, 182
   Chicken Curry with Spinach, Herbs and Cream/*Palak Murgh*, 50–51
   Saag Paneer/*Palak Paneer*, 148–9
   Spinach and Sultana Samosas, 172–7
   Spinach, Date and Spring Onion Raita/*Khajoor, Palak & Hara Pyaz Ka Raita*, 236–7

split peas: Rustic Yellow Split Pea Dal/*Tadka Dal*, 130–31
Star Anise Ice Cream/*Chakri Phool Ice Cream*, 256–7
Stuffed Potato Cakes/*Aloo Tikki*, 158–61
Sunil's Garlic Bread, 218–19
Sunil's Stir-Fried Vegetables/*Subz Miloni*, 178–9
Sweet Potato and Chickpea Curry with Rack of Lamb/*Bengali Babu's Chana Gosht*, 76–7
Sweet-and-Sour Aubergine Chutney/*Baingan Chutney*, 225–6
Sweet-and-Sour Pumpkin/*Khatta Meetha Kaddu*, 192–3
sweetcorn: Wild Mushrooms and Sweetcorn with Almonds/*Makai Khumbh Badam Ki Subzi*, 190–91

T

tandoori:
Tandoori Lamb Chops/*Gosht Ki Champain*, 66–7
  Tandoori-Style Chicken/*Tandoori Murgh*, 42–5
  Tandoori-Style Pineapple/*Kesari Ananas*, 248–9
tomatoes:
Home-Style Fish Curry with Vegetables/*Meen Curry*, 120–21
  Lamb Shanks with Tomatoes, Almonds and Yoghurt/*Nalli Ki Kaliya*, 84–5
  Tomato and Cashew Chutney/*Bengali Chutney*, 222–3
Turmeric Poached Pears/*Rasedar Nashpati*, 246–7

V

Vegetable Roll/*Kolkata Kathi Kebab*, 150–51

W

walnuts:
Ghai Sahib's Semolina Pudding/*Ghai Sahib Ka Suji Halwa*, 242–3
  Indian Rice Pudding/*Kheer*, 240–41
  Pear and Walnut Chutney/*Akhrot, Nashpati Ki Chutney*, 234–5
Warm Chickpea, Mango and Coconut Salad/*Sundal*, 166–7
Wild Mushrooms and Sweetcorn with Almonds/*Makai Khumbh Badam Ki Subzi*, 190–91
wraps: Vegetable Roll/*Kolkata Kathi Kebab*, 150–51

Y

yoghurt:
Lamb Shanks with Tomatoes, Almonds and Yoghurt/*Nalli Ki Kaliya*, 84–5
  Salmon with Yoghurt, Mustard and Turmeric/*Doi Maach*, 118–19
  Spiced Whole Roasted Cauliflower/*Gobhi Musallam*, 162–3
  Sweet-and-Sour Yoghurt, 158
see also lassi; raita

ACKNOWLEDGEMENTS

I have been wanting to write a cookbook for many years. Thank you to all the following people who helped to make this dream a reality.

To my chefs and all the team at Pickle, Tiffin and Street, especially for your help during the recipe testing and photo shoot. I couldn't do what I do without you all.

To my friend and manager Prasana for all your support and help.

To Michael McLoughlin and Patricia Deevy at Penguin Sandycove for giving me the opportunity to share my recipes with a wider audience. To editor Kristin Jensen for putting all the recipes down on the page and making sure they work for home cooks. To Clare Sayer for careful copy-editing. To Jo Murphy and Charlotte O'Connell for their excellent work photographing and styling the book. At Penguin, thanks to Saffron Stocker for her great design. And to Issy Hanrahan, Natalie Wall and Annie Underwood for making sure the book ended up between covers and in your hands.

To Darina Allen for inspiring me and encouraging me to write this book.

To all my customers in all the restaurants I've worked in over the years and at my own restaurants now. I value you so much.

To my wife, Leena, and son, Ishan, for supporting me while I worked on this book, especially to Leena for managing both Street and Tiffin so that I could concentrate on the book.

And to my mother, whose cooking and recipes were my first inspiration and whose food continues to inspire me today.

SANDYCOVE

UK | USA | Canada | Ireland | Australia
India | New Zealand | South Africa

Sandycove is part of the Penguin Random House group of companies whose addresses can be found at global.penguinrandomhouse.com.

First published 2023
001

Copyright © Sunil Ghai, 2023

The moral right of the author has been asserted

Photography © Joanne Murphy

Colour reproduction by Altaimage Ltd

Printed in Italy by Printer Trento s.r.l.

The authorized representative in the EEA is Penguin Random House Ireland, Morrison Chambers, 32 Nassau Street, Dublin D02 YH68

A CIP catalogue record for this book is available from the British Library

ISBN: 978-1-844-88583-1

FOOD IS A PERSONAL JOURNEY, one we are on for our whole lives. We can relive our happiest moments through the flavours of our childhood, and get to know people, cultures and places by exploring and sharing food experiences. On my journey as a chef and restaurateur, I have discovered new tastes, new relationships and new histories through food. And I have remembered, longed for and rediscovered those from my own past in India by recreating and reimagining those culinary memories for my family, friends and customers.

I'm originally from Gwalior, known as the 'Royal City', in northern India. The city's palaces were a draw for India's most talented chefs and to this day Gwalior has a rich food culture, especially street food. Growing up with food in this environment influenced my work as a chef, but what really drives me are my memories of my childhood family home, especially my mother's role at the heart of the family.

As is common in India, I grew up in a large extended family with my parents and siblings along with the families of my father's brothers.